MW00582635

A GUIDE TO COLLABORATIVE
COMMUNICATION FOR SERVICE-LEARNING
AND COMMUNITY ENGAGEMENT PARTNERS

A GUIDE TO COLLABORATIVE COMMUNICATION FOR SERVICE-LEARNING AND COMMUNITY ENGAGEMENT PARTNERS

Rebecca J. Dumlao

Foreword by Cathy Burack

STERLING, VIRGINIA

COPYRIGHT © 2018 BY STYLUS
PUBLISHING, LLC.

Published by Stylus Publishing, LLC 22883 Quicksilver Drive
Sterling, Virginia 20166-2019

All rights reserved. No part of this book may be reprinted or reproduced
in any form or by any electronic, mechanical, or other means, now
known or hereafter invented, including photocopying, recording, and
information storage and retrieval, without permission in writing from
the publisher.

Library of Congress Cataloging-in-Publication Data
Names: Dumlao, Rebecca J., 1955- author.
Title: A guide to collaborative communication for service-learning and
community engagement partners / Rebecca J. Dumlao ; foreword by
Cathy Burack.
Description: First edition. | Sterling, Virginia : Stylus Publishing, LLC.,
[2018] |
Includes bibliographical references and index.
Identifiers: LCCN 2018009951 (print) |
LCCN 2018026713 (ebook) |
ISBN 9781620361108 (mobi, e Pub) |
ISBN 9781620361092 (vPDF) |
ISBN 9781620361085 (pbk. : alk. paper) |
ISBN 9781620361078 (cloth : alk. paper) |
ISBN 9781620361092 (library networkable e-edition) |
ISBN 9781620361108 (consumer e-edition)
Subjects: LCSH: Communication in education. | Community and
school. | Service learning.
Classification: LCC LB1033.5 (ebook) |
LCC LB1033.5 .D96 2018 (print) |
DDC 371.102/2--dc23
LC record available at https://lccn.loc.gov/2018009951

13-digit ISBN: 978-1-62036-107-8 (cloth)
13-digit ISBN: 978-1-62036-108-5 (paperback)
13-digit ISBN: 978-1-62036-109-2 (library networkable e-edition)
13-digit ISBN: 978-1-62036-110-8 (consumer e-edition)

Printed in the United States of America

All first editions printed on acid-free paper that meets the American
National Standards Institute Z39-48 Standard.

Bulk Purchases
Quantity discounts are available for use in workshops and for
staff development.
Call 1-800-232-0223

First Edition, 2018

CONTENTS

FOREWORD

*The sharing of joy, whether physical, emotional, psychic, or intellectual, forms
a bridge between the sharers which can be the basis for understanding much of
what is not shared between them, and lessens the threat of their difference.*

—Audre Lorde

The author of this volume, like so many other authors, started writing this book several years before its publication. Rebecca J. Dumlao could not have known at the time she set out to rigorously investigate communication within service-learning and community engagement how needed and applicable *A Guide to Collaborative Communication for Service-Learning and Community Engagement Partners* would be today.

There is a longtime and continuing need to address the specific behaviors, skills, and knowledge that contribute to successful community-campus partnerships. Resources and research abound for those on the higher education side of the partnership equation. Faculty have guides on how to design their syllabi to include service, find resources within and about their disciplines, engage in scholarship, and disseminate and document their work for review. Campus administrators can find information on how to set up effective and sustainable structures that support an array of campus-wide community engagement initiatives and activities. And students, many of whom engaged in service-related activities in high school, can access campus resources that allow them to continue their community engagement in a variety of forms. The bulk of service-learning and community engagement research and resources includes mention of the "community" side of the partnership equation by explicating the *shoulds* of creating and maintaining community partnerships. For instance, the Foundational Indicators of the 2015 application for the Carnegie Elective Community Engagement Classification ask institutions to document the number and scope of community partnerships. Categories, based on best practices, include the *shoulds* of "mutuality and reciprocity, mechanisms to systematically collect and share feedback and assessment findings, and examples of faculty scholarship associated with outreach and partnership activities" (Campus Compact, 2016). Campus Compact's approach to good partnerships, as another example, includes "clear, common goals and ongoing communication, shared resources and mutual benefit; and mobilization of each partner's distinct assets" (Campus Compact, 2016). There is a burgeoning literature that is based on evaluating and researching the successes and challenges of specific community partnerships and the extent to which they employ the principles of good practice—the *shoulds*—which were described previously. However, there are far fewer resources that thoroughly address the *hows* of good practice—the ways to authentically and effectively bring the principles required for successful community-campus partnerships to life. And what about community partners? What resources and tools exist for them to engage with their higher education partner? The currently popular idiom "not so much" comes to mind. This volume powerfully addresses both the *shoulds* and the *hows* of what I believe is the central component of the success of any ongoing partnership or relationship—communication.

What makes *A Guide to Collaborative Communication for Service-Learning and Community Engagement Partners* even more compelling is that it is being published at a time in which most would agree that much of the U.S. cultural and political context is in need of an intervention. For a number of years I cofacilitated a think tank comprising chief student affairs officers from a variety of campuses in New England. The think tank's agenda included in-depth discussions of pressing issues within higher education. One of last year's topics was on the declining ability of students to engage in dialogue or constructive argument. These vice presidents and deans observed, as have I, that expressing a different point of view on an issue became a proxy for "you are either for me or against me." The consequences of this inability to engage with one another could be seen in students checking out of any conversation that might lead to conflict, students continuing to engage but feeling traumatized by doing so, and campuses struggling to hold on to their own sense of community. To quote a line from the film *Cool Hand Luke* (Carroll & Rosenberg, 1967), "What we've got here is failure to communicate." We see this inability to communicate replicated in our school board meetings, city councils, corporate work settings, and at the highest levels of our government. The timeliness of this volume is that Dumlao provides the antidote to our failure to communicate by tackling the requisite knowledge and attitudes head-on. Her emphasis on "collaborative communication" implies that effective communication requires specific skills and communication within the goal of sustaining a healthy partnership—whether in community, with another person, across a campus, or across the country—requires a collaborative approach that holds maintaining a relational perspective at its center. As Dumlao puts it, "The thinking that undergirds collaborative communication includes attention to the partnership (the 'we') as well as attention to the individual partner's needs/concerns (the 'me') to reach beyond both"

(p. 41, this volume). This is written from the perspective of one who is both a scholar and practitioner, who knows that issues of diversity, equity, and inclusion as well as differences in power and privilege, trust, context, and change permeate every relationship and left unaddressed can and will undermine collaborative communication and ultimately the partnership.

Like you, I want to make this world a better place. This volume gives me the tools I can use to do that. When I think about the ideal form of collaborative communication, it is about a way to share joy with others. We can and must do this.

Cathy Burack
Senior Fellow for Higher Education Center
for Youth and Communities
Brandeis University

ACKNOWLEDGMENTS

Writing this book has been a collaborative effort! Thanks to my East Carolina University (ECU) administrators, Chris Buddo, Linda Kean, Ron Michelson, Laura Prividera, and Chancellor Cecil Staton, for your unwavering support. Heartfelt praise goes to Angie Brown and Teresa Bullock for making it easy for me to travel by doing the detail work so well. Kudos go to my School of Communication faculty colleagues—they regularly demonstrate collaboration to support our students, programs, and each other. More times than I can count, Michael Cavanagh, John Howard, Sachiyo Shearman, Brittany Thompson, and Deborah Thomson listened thoughtfully to book ideas and offered encouragement. Thanks are inadequate. I could not have completed this multiyear project without you!

My students, face-to-face and online, have shown me how impactful service-learning and community-engaged scholarship can be for real people. You constantly remind me what really matters. Megan Gibson, grad assistant extraordinaire, planted the seed that led to the community puppet project. Kelley Deal, my student two different times, demonstrates often how to make a difference for others. Kala Godwin proved to be an insight-filled, awesome reader, writer, and editor for part of this book. Shayna and Teresa (and all student puppeteers) made the puppetry with children enriching for all. The many, many community partners working with my students and me taught us so very much. Names would fill multiple pages. I don't want to miss anyone. Just know, I have been honored (and changed) by working with each and every one of you.

Todd Fraley, Dennis McCunney, and Nichelle Shuck demonstrate wisdom and true commitment as they work with me to plan the upcoming service-learning study abroad program in Northern Ireland. Sharon Ballard, the late Linner Griffin, and members of ECU's Service-Learning Committee have consistently carried out caring, collaborative work to benefit many. Tara Kermiet ably helps us coordinate and carry out service-learning efforts across campus. Hunt McKinnon, Sharon Paynter, Robbie Quinn, Kirk St. Amant, Beth Velde, Beth Wall-Bassett, and others in ECU's Engagement and Outreach Scholars Academy continually raise the bar for what we can accomplish working with community experts. Eric Evans and Kenny Flowers serve as valuable role models for true collaboration. This book is richer because of all of you!

People with Campus Compact are doing excellent community-based work, too. Leslie Garvin serves as leader and cheerleader for so many of us in North Carolina. It was through Campus Compact that I first met Cathy Burack and learned about her far-reaching work. Cathy Hamilton, Emily Janke, and Spoma Jovanovic, at the University of North Carolina–Greensboro, are phenomenal community collaborators. Thanks, Emily, for your "partnership identity" idea that informs my work, as well as for introducing me to Kathleen Edwards, who in turn introduced me to Isiahm and Gwen. Storyscapes and other community engagement work by champions around the world inspire me far deeper than I can say. Please know how grateful I am to all of you for sharing so openly.

Sincere thanks to Kent Koth and others at Seattle University for welcoming me back to the Pacific Northwest. Your work in collaboration with Bailey Gatzert Elementary School is life changing. Sally Haber, Grel Imel, and Seattle Youth Initiative participants, please accept my deep gratitude for showing me your community-focused work in action!

John von Knorring proved to be a very patient publisher. While some of his advice was hard to hear, he was always on point and very kind. Not all publishing experiences are like this. You represent the very best!

Amara and Makana Dumlao, Keri Dixon; Charlie, Debbie, Kelsey, and Taylor Cherry; and my doggies, Nani and Dolce, make up the family that give me ongoing life support (haha) and love. Jodi Hudson, while technically not family, communicates so often with me that I might have to grant her honorary family membership. Robin Blomquist has been my dear friend since high school and has always supported this writing and me. Thanks everybody for listening to me talk about this book, and for always lifting me up! I love you all.

Above my desk is a single word: *Inspire*. My hope is that each person listed—and all the readers—will be inspired to positively work with people in our communities, near and far, to solve problems and address big issues together. This collaborative communication work matters. So do each of you!

INTRODUCTION

*Never doubt that a small group of thoughtful citizens can change
the world; indeed, it is the only thing that ever has.*

—Margaret Mead

To create a brighter future, people *must* come together to address today's big challenges. We face issues like divergent student access to education, changing business environments, health disparities, crime, environmental changes, homelessness, hunger, inequalities among groups, violence, and much more (Boyer, 1994; Fitzgerald, Allen, & Roberts, 2010; Siegel, 2010). None of us has *all* the knowledge and capabilities to solve these complex problems alone, but together we can make transformative changes that build a better world.

Working collaboratively is an idea whose time has come. Still, even though we all have a general idea about what *collaboration* means, actually "doing" collaboration or "being collaborative" involves a paradigm shift in the ways we think, interact, and work with each other.

Different Ways to Work Together

Picture one variety of working together as a pyramid with those individuals at the top coming up with a master plan. Those farther on down would be expected to implement that vision, step-by-step. In contrast, imagine interlocking circles of people inventing a new dream and deciding what needs to be done as a group. Each person would contribute knowledge and abilities to create the desired end result.

No doubt, there are other possibilities for working together than these two extremes depict. Even so, this vivid contrast illustrates distinctions between a hierarchical approach and a collaborative approach to partnering. Interestingly enough, the shift toward more collaboration is now happening on campuses, in communities, and in some businesses, as well as many other places in our increasingly interconnected world.

Here's how collaboration might work in a community-campus partnership: Consider a college student who wants to build a playground for children in an area where there is no good place to play. Using the traditional orientation to working together, the student could lead efforts to raise money, work through needed paperwork or permits, create the design, and get it done. Other people might help with various tasks to get the park built. The finished park might be good *for* the community children and their families—or not!

Although this approach is common, it is not necessarily the best choice for those being "served." Children could play on the equipment, but parents and other community members might not like the equipment selected, the way the playground was designed, or where it was located. Truth is, the community members were not involved in creating and building the park and consequently may not take ownership of the finished park at all.

In contrast, the student and campus representatives could set up a meeting with community members to brainstorm ideas for the new park. People from the community, including children, could share ideas about what they want. Experts could take the ideas, render design drawings, and provide construction plans. Children and parents could raise funds alongside college students. Others could work with government officials to secure permits. Everybody could help with construction. Using this approach the student and campus representatives would work in harmony *with* the community members—collaborating from start to finish of the new park.

This collaborative approach can work well. My own two children helped build a park near their elementary school this way. The children brainstormed ideas and drawings for what they wanted in the park with the architect. They also cleverly collected enough pennies to cover the gym floor to help pay for the project. Parents and others in the community got permits and completed other tasks. Then on workdays, everybody in the community, including the college football team, built the structures. When it was done, the entire community *owned* that park. Each person involved held many great memories about working together to construct the unique playground, too.

About This Book

This book homes in on partnership at the most basic level of interaction—between two people as they work toward common goals. Barbara Holland (2005) says, "This very personal level of connection is where most community partners feel some confidence there will be reciprocity, trust, and respect for their perspectives" (p. 11). The interpersonal dynamics described in this book are equally valid for formal and institutional relationships between members of a community or community organization and representatives from campus. In other words, when two people connect, regardless of their respective roles and responsibilities, they can use the collaborative communication principles and practices found here to build flexible, lasting relationships that will weather most challenges.

So learning about relationships and collaboration between two partners is a great place to start to create a brighter future for our communities! Large-scale partnerships such as those between groups or institutions rely on healthy, effective relationships between individuals as well (see more at Bringle, Clayton, & Price, 2009).

This book also offers a conceptual framework of collaborative communication to build and sustain partnerships. Fostering healthy, mostly positive relationships using collaborative communication isn't a onetime endeavor. Communication processes that work at one time in the relationship will undoubtedly change as the people involved and the circumstances change. That's why this book defines *collaborative communication* as a repertoire of knowledge and skills allowing partners to make choices that fit the situation or context. Some of the tools in that repertoire will involve face-to-face communication; others may involve social media like Twitter, Facebook, Instagram, or Snapchat. But the end goals will consistently be focused on relational communication that helps, not hurts, the partners (and others involved) and also forwards their community work.

Specifically, the framework and the book pinpoint communication knowledge and strategies that can help partners, including the following:

- Connect and build trusting, effective relationships.
- Converse in ways that participants are heard and understood.
- Envision the possibilities of what can be done together.
- Commit to one another and to the joint work and then create solutions.
- Understand partner patterns that make this relationship unique.

Together, these elements help individuals collaborate using distinct communication processes and practices, even while working through differences and challenges along the way.

The elements can work together to help partners move skillfully between the "we" with the collective insights or actions and the "me" with the individual-level expertise, experience, and contributions. Partners can recycle through various elements of collaborative communication as needed across the lifetime of the partnership.

This book is written for partners focused on community engagement, including service-learning, in the United States and in other parts of the world. This practical guide could be used for preparing college students to work more effectively in the community. It could be used in workshops for community and campus members who work with service-learning students. It could be used in professional development workshops held at academic conferences, through continuing education, or in a community setting. Much content could also be useful to scholars, students, or community members involved in community-engaged research.

What's in the Chapters

Chapter 1 follows the old but true adage "Know thyself." In this chapter, you will consider key influences on you that significantly impact your communication with others. Chapter 2 delves into partnership communication more deeply, highlighting what's needed for effective community engagement relationships like service-learning, extended volunteer efforts, and community-based research. This chapter also recaps foundational contemporary ideas about communication from expert sources. Chapter 3 presents the innovative collaborative communication framework that can help you organize your communication-related thoughts and practices as you move through various natural stages in your partnerships. Some of the variations in collaboration are covered as well as times when collaboration might not be the best option. Chapter 4 specifies practices and processes that you can use to build collaborative communication and healthy, sustainable partnerships in real life. Chapter 5 covers leadership communication practices for readers—no matter what roles they currently hold in the community-based partnership. *Community engagement work*, defined as a type of collaboration between partners, encourages everyone to assume some leadership roles and to develop new leadership capabilities. Chapter 6 spells out important communication knowledge and best practices for navigating cultural differences while supporting collaborative relationships. Chapter 7 addresses the topic of managing the conflicts that will naturally arise in your partnerships. You will be encouraged to learn more about your partner and your situation using different communication processes so you can make decisions together about how to proceed. (Some cautions are also offered about what may be needed for healthy relationships, including when the partners need help to work together.) Chapter 8 focuses on creative ways to partner and to celebrate the partnership and accomplishments along the way. Taking delight in one another through "nurture norms" and related practices can help build long-lasting relationships. This chapter also identifies trends for community engagement in the future and offers insights about ways collaborative communication can foster meaningful change.

The appendix offers specific activities to build your collaborative communication repertoire, either alone or with others. This is followed by a useful annotated bibliography of resources to consult as you develop your collaboratively focused partnership. In other words, the bibliography gives you more information about ideas in the book.

Throughout the book, real-world examples and community stories are offered to bring key concepts to life. The shorter illustrative examples are based on experience. The lengthy stories at the end of select chapters involved recorded face-to-face interviews by the author. Participants reviewed and approved each story before being added to this book.

By reading this book and applying the content in your own community-campus work, you are embarking on a journey that will have its ups and downs. That's to be expected! Relationship-building doesn't happen all at once. There are likely to be multiple surprises along the way. But do keep at it. The benefits for the community—and for you—can be some of the most rewarding you will ever experience!

THINKING ABOUT
OURSELVES AND OUR
PARTNERSHIPS

What lies behind us and what lies before us are tiny matters compared to what lies within us.

—Author Unknown

As we endeavor to promote positive change for others in our communities, we must start by looking at ourselves. What we find there will have a profound impact on what we can do while working with others. Our choices for how we will interact are shaped by past experiences and the patterns of thinking that define us. We can also make changes, if we so choose.

From the time we are young, each of us develops perceptions about who we are that reflect beliefs, attitudes, and values. Long ago, Cooley (1902) noted that we develop our self-concepts as if looking at ourselves through a looking glass or mirror. As we think about ourselves, this metaphorical mirror reflects back to us ways the important people in our lives perceive and evaluate us as well as our own internal responses (McCornack, 2013, p. 41).

To illustrate, Johann had a muscular body, light-colored hair, and distinctive facial features. He learned from his parents that he was expected to be strong, to participate in athletics, and to support people in his neighborhood no matter what. Over time, Johann's self-concept was so shaped by his parents' influence that he no longer thought about being a strong, athletic guy deeply committed to others. Those things were all part of who he was.

Our ideas about ourselves are much more complex than this example, though—we have many layers of self. In the children's movie *Shrek* (Warner, Williams, Katzenberg, Adamson, & Jenson, 2001), the lead character is an ogre named Shrek. He uses an onion metaphor to describe himself to his

7

donkey friend. Shrek says, "There's a lot more to ogres than people think
. . . . Onions have layers—OGRES have layers" (quoted in McCornack,
2013, pp. 58–59).

People also have layers! The outer layers include numerous factors like
age, college major, hometown, or occupation. Many of these features are
obvious or readily shared with others. But deeper layers hold our core values, fears, self-concepts, and distinctive personality traits that make us one
of a kind (see Altman & Taylor, 1973). These core layers are invisible and,
usually, not quickly shared with new people we meet.

Still, the various layers of self influence our thinking when we interact
with one another. For instance, Johann's ingrained tendencies to help his
community would likely lead him to listen carefully to a neighbor's needs,
think about ways he could help, and then offer assistance.

Thoughts about oneself might also impact initial interactions between
a community partner and a student. Consider the case of Shannon, who
was the director of the Teddy Bear Center. He really wanted to encourage
students to get involved with the children, so he contacted a nearby campus
to explore possibilities. Soon he was surprised to find out that students were
contacting him directly far more than he had anticipated.

For instance, Rachel, a college senior, called and wanted to set up a quick
Skype conversation with Shannon before completing her service-learning
hours. Shannon didn't want to Skype. He was uncomfortable with virtual
communication and was annoyed that Rachel was in such a hurry.

Initially, that's all they knew. However, because he really wanted to have
students come help out, Shannon called Rachel back the next day suggesting
that they talk via phone to determine next steps. During that conversation,
they uncovered significant differences in thinking. Rachel's thoughts and sharing centered on her life as an employed college student with a family and a full
course load. She was concerned about how she could complete required hours
working with children with disabilities at the Teddy Bear Center in addition
to everything else. Rachel let Shannon know that she was comfortable using
Skype because she regularly used it to converse with family members overseas.

In contrast, Shannon explained that the center worked with children
who were abused, not children with disabilities. Skype would not allow him
to ask questions about Rachel's motivations and to assess her capabilities
fully. He said he needed to meet in person to discuss training requirements,
strategies for working with the children, privacy concerns, and required
paperwork. Shannon also pointed out how much he hoped to involve college students at the center because they helped the children do activities that
the staff just could not do given other responsibilities.

Clearly, these two held different bases for their thinking that led them to draw different conclusions. In the end, Rachel took a different placement that semester, working with children with physical limitations. Shannon agreed this other placement would be a better fit.

Still, they created a good rapport that left the door open for future work together. Shannon knew he'd created a good rapport with a student that could yield future possibilities for the center. Rachel was also happy. She liked Shannon and could see real value for her career by working at the Teddy Bear Center when her life was less hectic.

Thinking About Our World

It's not just ideas about ourselves that influence our thinking. Over our entire lives, we develop strong connections between ideas and emotions that form well-worn pathways in our brains. In other words, repetitious thought patterns chart the ways we think most readily. For example, our big-picture perspective, known as a worldview, results from oft-rehearsed thoughts. This worldview shapes our outlook across a wide variety of situations.

A *worldview* can be defined as "an encompassing picture of reality based on a set of assumptions about how the world works" (Lavenda & Schultz, 2010, p. 68). Our worldview is heavily shaped by individual tendencies, experiences with our families, cultures we represent, and other background influences. Importantly, our own worldviews influence *all* our interactions—including the content we think is important to talk about and the ways we characteristically interact with others!

For a real-life example of people with two culturally distinct worldviews and how those views influenced their communication, consider Gracie and Larry. Gracie learned from an early age to be resourceful and fix things herself rather than to call in a repairman. Her mother took great pride in coming up with thrifty solutions to address everyday inconveniences; she passed this innovativeness on to her daughter.

Later, as an adult, Gracie lived on her own in Florida and followed those well-learned patterns. Her landlord, Larry, was perplexed, though, by the way she used things like superglue to fix the plumbing or twine to hold a door with a broken hinge in place. Larry much preferred to increase the value of his property by calling in someone with expertise to make permanent repairs using brand-new parts.

At first, Gracie was really confused about why Larry wanted to spend so much money on things that could be managed for much less. But, as they talked, she realized that not only did Larry have money to pay for any repairs but also his approach made long-term financial and pragmatic sense.

Their frank conversations about their reasoning for actions helped them both learn about individual worldviews regarding home maintenance. The next spring, when Gracie worked with her classmates to build a Habitat for Humanity house, what she had learned while talking with Larry became even more meaningful.

Thinking About "Me" and "We"

By definition, *community engagement work* depends on partnerships between people to meet a need or address a concern in a community, either locally or at a distance (e.g., through a partnership with an organization in another country). Further, this community engagement work involves shifting from "me" to "we" in our thinking.

In the United States, many of us have been encouraged to value the American Dream of independence, individual initiative, and striving to succeed through our own efforts. Those perspectives are valuable in many situations. Yet the seemingly opposite values of mutual benefit, mutual dependence, interdependence, and reciprocity are essential to sustained community partnerships (Bringle & Hatcher, 2002; Brinkerhoff, 2002; Carriere, 2008; Holland, 2005) and to collaboration (Hardy, Lawrence, & Grant, 2005; Heath & Frey, 2004; Lewis, 2006; Walker & Stohl, 2012). At first glance, then, when we do community engagement we seem to be shifting from a heavy focus on the individual or one person ("me") toward a focus on the whole or many people ("we") as we work with others in communities.

But becoming more "we" focused isn't the whole picture. Instead, in community-based work and in collaboration more generally, we must become skilled at transitioning back and forth between "me" and "we" depending on what is most needed at the time.

Think about how both "me" and "we" perspectives are needed to address environmental pollution, an important local and global problem. One scientist can provide expertise on how different factors interact to create a pollution problem that extends beyond one location. An educator can demonstrate ways to cut down on waste—to reduce, reuse, and recycle. The local trash collector can provide recycle bins. And so on. These individual people, each one a "me," are needed to make meaningful changes to address this problem. They also need to work together (to use the "we" perspective) to progress toward a lasting solution.

As another example, consider the importance of the "me" and "we" in developing research so both the study and the results are meaningful for not only the research team but also members of the community. Becca, a researcher/teacher, was interested in using puppets to teach at-risk children about healthy eating. She knew how to do interviews effectively (using "me" expertise), but she didn't know what parents wanted their children to eat or what the children usually ate (the "we" expertise).

Her community partner, Shena, wasn't sure she wanted to approve a research project. In the past, many academics had come to her community agency to do research. All too often, once the research was published there was no further contact with people in the community. So, from Shena's viewpoint, the research benefited the scholars but not the people she knew and worked with every day.

It took a lot of frank sharing before Shena and Becca realized that they shared a deep interest in teaching the children healthier eating patterns. Becca asked Shena what she wanted to know about the children's eating habits and how she would like to find that out. Shena said, "It would be really interesting to talk with parents about what they want their children to eat that would be more nutritious." Then they talked about using puppets to share new messages with young children as a great way to gain and keep their attention.

So Becca and her research team member put together a set of questions to ask verbally and reviewed it with Shena for suggested changes. After they agreed on the questions, Shena invited parents to come to the community center one evening. The team interviewed parents to gather information for new puppetry scripts to use with children in the community.

What everyone learned this way could certainly not have been discovered in an isolated office on campus. Instead, the team enacted core community engagement values like trust, reciprocity, mutual benefit, and power sharing by working together (as a "we") with the parents before, during, and after the study.

Notably, ideas of "me" and "we" show up through the language and actions people use as they talk with one another. Sometimes it is important to focus on the "we," what we can do together as we talk. But other times, it may be more important to focus on "me," to share one's own perceptions, skills, and expertise, or to fully represent one's own organization. Learning what kind of talk is needed in different scenarios and with different people is highly valuable. (You'll find a collaboration checklist in the appendix and more ideas throughout the book.)

Thinking About Relationships

Although individual thoughts, thinking patterns, and related conversations are important, a more macro perspective is needed to think effectively about long-term, sustainable partnerships. The communication tone and impact of single interactions sum up over time, building a "relational climate" and a "relational culture" between partners. This matters—a lot!

Relational climate refers to the snap judgments we make about how well a relationship is working. You do this when you think about your best friend and how great it was to see her last weekend. The fun time you had together set a positive tone for the next time you'll see each other, so your quick assessment is that your "relational climate" is positive. You look forward eagerly to the next time you'll meet with this friend.

Researchers tell us that specific ratios of positive to negative interactions, as perceived by each partner, predict the long-term success of a relationship. Gottman (1993) found through lab-based research that a five-to-one positivity ratio is needed for marital success. That means that five positive snap judgments are needed for every one that is more negative in order for the marriage to thrive. Similarly, Frederickson (2009) found that experiencing positive feelings at a minimum of three-to-one was necessary for flourishing in other relationships. Interestingly enough, some communication scholars study *positive communication.* This is defined as "message processes that display pro-social, ethical, spiritual/religious, and positive character qualities" (Socha & Pitts, 2012, p. 12) in order to find ways to benefit relational partners or their relationship over time, all the while recognizing that partners can (and will) face challenges along the way.

The other term mentioned, *relational culture,* is defined as "a private world of rules, understandings, meanings and patterns of acting and interpreting that partners create for their relationship" (Wood, 2007, p. 308). The unique relational culture between partners is like an unwritten but well-understood guidebook for how they interact. These guides are developed through multiple shared experiences and conversations. Some idiosyncratic meanings—held just between the two people in the relationship—will be developed in the process.

Your relationship history with your best friend, for instance, allows you to know what to expect. You know, for instance, that you can expect your friend to be excited when something good happens to you. You also know she will use the special gesture, hands in quick applause, the next time she sees you via Skype or in person to let you know she cherishes and celebrates your success.

Experts recognize that relationships can be significantly impacted not only by the words used and the content being shared between partners but also by the way information is shared. In short then, relational cultures don't just happen but are created by those involved. (More specifics about relational communication are offered later in the book.)

Thinking About Trust

Trust, an emotionally based set of cognitions, also develops over time and reflects the experiences of the partners. Reina and Reina (2006) say, "Effective relationships are built on trust; if you don't have trust, you don't have much of a relationship" (p. 154). One type of trust known as contractual trust involves "a mutual understanding that people in the relationship will do what they say they will do" (p. 16).

Here's how that works. You know, for instance, you can trust your community member, Anna, to get her part of the e-mail newsletter done on time, just like she said she would do. Similarly, the local food kitchen director, Tomas, trusts that students will come as scheduled to serve meals. Tomas counts on each one to keep his or her word and be there to help. Both relationships work because of contractual trust. (Find more about trust in chapter 4.)

Thinking About Collaboration

Collaboration is growing in importance far beyond our community-engaged work. Lewis (2006) points out, "Collaboration is likely to be a hallmark of the century. We see calls for it in nearly every aspect of life and a need for it in many contexts" (p. 241). Also, "in most communities today, it is a necessity for groups, organizations, and institutions to work together collaboratively to confront complex issues" (Heath & Frey, 2004, p. 189). So learning about collaboration is something that can benefit you now as well as in the future.

We know collaboration is a positive, innovative way to interact with communities and to address social problems, but we still have a lot to learn about how to do it well (see Keyton & Stallworth, 2003). Even so, in her extensive interdisciplinary review of literature, Lewis (2006) identified five common or convergent features in articles about effective collaboration.

First, collaboration typically focuses on action and doing. "We don't have a collaboration, nor are we a collaboration; *we engage in collaboration*" (Lewis, 2006, p. 213). So you can think of collaboration as a "way of doing" (p. 213) things that is "fundamentally communicative" (p. 242). Or, Heath and Frey (2004) put it like this: "Communication . . . is more than a tool used" by collaborators; "it is constitutive of community collaboration" (p. 225). In other words, communication is integral in forming and maintaining collaborative efforts between community-campus partners.

You'll learn a lot more about collaborative communication and build a whole repertoire of practices and processes for partnering throughout this book. But, for now, remember the research team described earlier? In that example, the "way of doing" research involved in-depth communication among Shena, Becca, the rest of the research team, and the parents. Together they talked about what to include in puppetry scripts and why so that the puppeteers could educate the children in ways that were sensitive to their needs, eating habits, and community cultures.

Second, Lewis (2006) found that collaboration is typically seen through a relational lens (p. 213), with a focus on positive regard for one another in terms of perceptions and behaviors (p. 219). This is similar to the "we" perspective and the ideas of relational climate and relational culture explained earlier in this chapter.

Emmy Award–winning journalist Kare Anderson (2014b) has coined the phrase "mutuality mind-set" to acknowledge that "we can be greater together than apart." That is, Anderson recognizes that although we have our independent needs and pursuits, we can also contribute to mutual purposes. This takes regular thinking about what works for us together, as partners or as a team. Moreover, the mutuality mind-set helps us to think about how our independent actions, as well as our joint work, might impact the partnership. Interestingly enough, Lewis (2006) also points out that "reciprocally interdependent" (p. 202) partners must mutually adjust rather than just having one person consistently change. So our thoughts reflecting the mutuality mind-set are likely to be dynamic, not static.

While using a mutuality mind-set, Anderson urges us to learn ways to become opportunity-makers with and for one another. In community-engaged settings, building opportunities for one another can spill over into innovative ways to address problems and meet our long-term goals.

A story might help explain how this works. Angel worked with the local soup kitchen and campus food efforts as a VISTA volunteer right after her graduation. While serving meals and coordinating campus efforts to use left-over food, she found her passion. She loved working in the community with the soup kitchen and the other people involved; this was more satisfying than anything else she had ever done.

The soup kitchen's director, Augusto, noticed her excitement. He told her about a new paid position as the director of a local community garden (thereby becoming an opportunity-maker for Angel). Her background in nutrition and dietetics along with her familiarity with the community made her perfect for the job. She could not only help in the garden but also demonstrate new ways to cook and serve the produce. Further, people in the community already trusted her so they enthusiastically recommended her. As a result of her connections, background, and experience, Angel got the job. She loved her new position and was very thankful that she'd met Augusto. In turn, he was glad he was able to provide Angel with an opportunity that continued to benefit the community. He was really glad he could regularly keep in touch with her. This was a win-win!

Third, Lewis (2006) involves equalizing the partners as they work together collaboratively. Equality may be sought in terms of roles, status, value/respect for different expertise, or varied contributions (p. 219). Also, collaborative communication processes may help equalize people so that all participants' wisdom, knowledge, concerns, and ideas become part of the decision-making process (p. 219). Because there are different ways for community-campus partners to feel that they are being treated equally, equality is an important discussion topic for partners to hold at different times across their relationship.

As an example, consider Sarah, a local animal center director, who wanted to be fully involved as a community partner with the service-learning class. She hoped that the professor would allow her to help educate the students by telling them more about what it was like to be part of an organization finding homes for abused animals. (This was a way for her to be an "equal" partner with the faculty member.) Sarah also hoped it would be possible to increase the number of student volunteers coming to work at the center after the class was over.

Sarah talked with the professor, Dr. Aaron, and soon discovered that he was amenable to her working as a coteacher as long as she recognized and respected his expertise in animal physiology. Together, they created an equitable partnership as coteachers for that semester's students. Their equitable partnership was so successful that they looked forward to future opportunities to address student learning as well as to meet the animal shelter's volunteer needs.

Fourth, Lewis (2006) found that collaborative partners emphasize the "process" rather than the end "product" or "accomplishment." Further, "different expected behaviors and roles (may) need to be fulfilled at different points" as the collaborative partnership is "expected to develop or change over time" (p. 220). Stated differently, the way a partnership (or partners) worked at one point may be quite different from the way the partnership works at another time or in a different situation.

As an example of a collaborative emphasis on process, consider the experience of Maisey, a grad student, who was excited to work as a research assistant to Dr. Aaron at the animal shelter. She planned to survey volunteers at the shelter to learn more about what motivated them. Her intended first step in survey development was to review the literature. But the shelter director, Sarah, wouldn't have it! Sarah wanted to know why volunteers were excited about their work but didn't want their responses to be based upon some theory or writings from people who didn't "do the work." This difference initially created major tension among Maisey, Dr. Aaron, and Sarah.

Subsequently, because they all wanted to do the right thing for the animals, they held a meeting to discuss the situation and invited a small group of dedicated volunteers to join in. The volunteers who attended suggested a series of conversations with other volunteers (i.e., focus groups) that they could lead. They also agreed with the researchers that planning some questions ahead of time would start the ball rolling. But, after that, the volunteers thought the conversations should emerge spontaneously, led only gently by Maisey and Dr. Aaron from the sidelines. By the end of this meeting with the key volunteers, everybody was enthusiastic about what they might learn together as the research progressed.

This group meeting proved to be a turning point, revitalizing the relationships between people from the shelter and from campus. Conflict quickly dissipated and the partnership moved forward with new energy. Once the focus groups were held a few weeks later, Sarah was able to create new recruiting publicity that increased the number of involved volunteers at the shelter from both on and off campus. And after the focus group data was gathered and analyzed, Maisey and Dr. Lewis looked at the literature to see how this new work might relate to what other academics had found previously in similar situations. They also worked to write a newsletter article with Sarah that might share important findings with the community. That way, everyone got what he or she needed to move forward. (See more about milestones and turning points in the exercises at the end of the chapter.)

Fifth, Lewis (2006) tells us collaboration is something that is volitional, informal, and emergent. Partners "own" a collaboration and freely "self-organize" or "construct" (p. 220) the collaboration through their actions. In other words, in collaboration, the partners themselves have ongoing responsibility to reorganize or redefine the partnership, so that goals can be accomplished while maintaining positive relationships as situations or people change. Still, sometimes choices other than collaboration may be beneficial in terms of appropriateness and effectiveness when voluntary collaboration is limited by circumstances or contexts outside the individual partners' control (see Lewis, 2006, pp. 232–235).

Interestingly enough, Janke (2009) found that community-campus partners can construct a *partnership identity*, defined as how campus representatives and community partners perceive who we are in this partnership over time. Once a partnership identity is formed, partners see themselves as being joined through the relationship instead of being separate people working together. The partnership identity they create is new and important to each of them, a part of how they now define themselves.

Final Thoughts for the Chapter

Thinking about our world, our partnerships, our collaborative work, and ourselves is complicated but essential to making positive community-focused changes. Partners can fully expect to talk about their joint work and their relationship all throughout the time they work together (see Bringle & Hatcher, 2002). There's a lot to learn from each other!

Hopefully, the tools in this book will help you as you continue to think, communicate, and act in partnership with others. As you read, keep in mind this truth: *Our individual communication choices reflect who we are and powerfully convey what we might do as we work collaboratively with others.*

Spotlight: Edgecombe County-East Carolina University Partnership Story

"If you take all the people of Edgecombe County, they've got needs, they've got problems, and they've got wants. They need jobs," states Eric Evans, assistant county manager of Edgecombe County, North Carolina. "We've got one of the highest unemployment rates, we've got high breast cancer mortality rates, and we've got everything that you would not want to be associated with your county."

Edgecombe County is one of the most distressed counties in the state. But that hasn't stopped Kenny Flowers, assistant vice chancellor of community and regional development at East Carolina University (ECU) and Evans from working on large-scale transformations. Together, they have fostered multiple community-campus partnerships and forged linkages to new state resources.

The two met and became friends years prior when each held other positions. Their relationship was revitalized when Flowers drove 25 miles across rural roads to see Evans and ask, "How can we help?"

"We started having conversations about how we diversify our local economy," noted Evans. Flowers encouraged Evans to take a grant-writing course and apply for grants to build local tourism. Related projects followed. One involved working with a professor and students on a site development plan for Shiloh Landing. This riverfront plantation once brokered slaves coming from ships so they could be sold nearby. The site plan preserved, honored, and shared that local history with contemporary visitors.

No matter where he works, Flowers tries to be sure that the community wants to collaborate. "A recipe for disaster in collaborative efforts is one or more party in that partnership not being really, really on board," he says. "The best advice I could give someone . . . is to be willing to listen first. And listen second. If you can listen and respond, your partners are much more likely to do the same thing."

It's also important, says Evans, to manage expectations about what the university can realistically do. "We take what you teach us. What you model for us. Then we share it." For instance, Evans learned how to draw a logic model to flush out ideas for grants.

"Before you go set up a meeting with somebody at the university, sit down and have a meeting with yourself. Think through what you want." He now draws a logic model to identify the most important need that impacts other needs. When a new partnership meeting starts, Evans refers back to this model so he can "just say that."

"Being willing to go to bat for your partner is key in building outstanding partnerships as opposed to base-level partnerships," says Flowers. "You have that connection. You have that investment. You have that ownership to the point that you are eager to go to bat" for your partner. That's the kind of long-term commitment strong partnerships can develop.

"You've got to have the long view," says Evans. "We can get some quick wins. But we also understand that there's a bigger payoff" that we might not be around to realize. "Big changes and transformations may not occur immediately."

Flowers wants to make sure each community partner knows that "there's not a reason ever that you shouldn't be able to stop by and have a conversation or pick up the phone and call. . . . Open communication is key."

Evans agrees. "Great work," he says, "starts at good people sitting down around a table. . . . Once we get to the table we talk about what I want and what you want, what you can do, what I can do, what we can do together. That's where it all starts." Thankfully, for them, "it just kept rolling."

Author's Note: When Hurricane Matthew came to eastern North Carolina in 2017, Edgecombe County was hit extremely hard. For the second time in just over a decade, the county faced massive flooding, family displacement, and community devastation. ECU provost Ron Mitchelson turned to Evans and Flowers to mobilize the campus. Busses of faculty, staff, and student volunteers traveled to Tarboro and Princeville to respond. So the communication, connectivity, and partnership between Evans and Flowers continue to make a difference.

Putting Chapter Ideas Into Action

Action for Partnerships and Teaching About Partnerships

1. Celebrating partnership successes through the course of the collaborative work can be motivating and help build positivity that partners

need to carry on their work. Pause now to think about turning points or important milestones in a partnership you are currently in or have experienced. (Turning points involve changing the partnership to get past a roadblock, potentially springboarding partners into innovative approaches that respond to the situation more effectively. Milestones are important accomplishments partners have achieved together.) Partners can independently (or together) identify turning points and milestones. Then these accomplishments can be used to celebrate the partnership—a great way to continue the momentum needed for sustained work.

2. Knowing where your partnership currently stands is important as you work together. For instance in a book by Mattessich, Murray-Close, and Monsey (2001), you'll find the Wilder Collaboration Factors Inventory. Take the test and look at your own results and the results of your partner. Use these results to have a conversation about your current partnership and what might lie ahead. (*Note*: You can also use the collaborative communication framework found in Table 3.1 to guide a conversation with a partner about your partnership and what might need work or how you might proceed in the future.)

Action for Community-Engaged Scholarship

1. Turning points can be important in developing lasting partnerships. Scholars and practitioners may want to study turning points in different community-engaged relationships to find commonalities or distinctions. Identifying key turning points in relationships could be vital to learn about change processes necessary for sustained community partnerships.

2. Collaboration and trust have been identified as important to partnerships generally, and to community engagement partnerships specifically. Research could help us learn how to best collaborate or how to establish the kinds of trust needed to move partnerships forward. Some research questions include the following: What kinds of trust are most needed between individual partners? What varieties of trust are needed between institutions or organizations that work together? What best practices can be identified for establishing and building trust?

3. Community-engaged research could help us understand the levels of positivity that may be needed for success in community-campus partnerships. A threshold level of positivity may be necessary to sustain a partnership over time, but this idea needs to be tested further by empirical research.

2

COMMUNITY ENGAGEMENT AND PARTNERSHIP COMMUNICATION

Be the change you wish to see in the world.

—Mahatma Gandhi

Those powerful words of Mahatma Gandhi still ring true today. As Nunn (2012) points out, you don't have to be a celebrity, a wealthy person, or a politician to start transforming your world. People like Martin Luther King Jr., Mother Teresa, Jonas Salk, and Clara Barton all made positive changes starting from scratch. None of them held elected office or ran corporations or made millions of dollars. Instead, they made huge differences for others because they cared enough to get involved.

You can be the change as well! And you don't need to work alone. Colleges and universities worldwide are becoming more community engaged, with campus representatives working with others in communities to solve pressing local problems and address unmet needs. On some campuses there are offices to coordinate these efforts. That's one place you can go as a student or community representative to learn more about what's happening now or to pitch your ideas about what could happen. You can also work with professors or through campus organizations to respond to issues that matter to you.

Pause now and ask yourself, "What community problem or issue creates such a strong response in me that I need to do something more about it?" It's a lot easier to stay involved with something that resonates deeply within us. Our passions can carry us forward and keep us committed even when we are delving into new, uncharted possibilities for our communities and facing the challenges that come up along the way.

What Is Community Engagement Anyway?

In this book, *community engagement* is an umbrella term that covers multiple forms of collaborative efforts between campuses and communities such as service-learning, community-engaged research/scholarship, and sustained volunteering. Each of these possibilities for community engagement will be discussed in this chapter so you can distinguish among them.

For instance, a community-engaged partnership focused on academic service-learning involves college students taking a class to address human and community needs, using structured reflections to promote learning (Jacoby, 1996, p. 5). Service-learning course objectives specifically involve working with community members and then relating those experiences back to course topics. Reflecting is how connections are made cognitively and involves writing or speaking or acting about ways community experiences inform the course topics, build community knowledge, or change the students personally or professionally.

To take one example of academic service-learning, in Aimee's Media and Culture course, college students learned about stereotypes presented on television and the Internet. Their professor, Dr. Thomas, set up a service-learning project so students could carry their learning off campus to share related information with children at a local Boys & Girls Club.

Before the students went anywhere, Kathy and Nathan, representatives from the club, came to class to talk about their work and the children. Nathan shared specific examples of how children at the club talked about "people like me" based on what they saw or heard in the media. All too often, said Kathy, the children described negative portrayals, limited opportunities, and biased language, especially about people of color, recent immigrants, or those with lower incomes. A frank, extended interaction ensued; the college students gradually realized that sharing positive images and possibilities would be an important contribution they could make for children at the club.

Kathy and Nathan also suggested a preliminary "get acquainted" visit so the students could meet, interact, and play with children at the club before developing materials to share with them later. So, after working out scheduling details with Kathy, Nathan, and Dr. Thomas, the students visited the center and started to build relationships with the children.

Next, back in the classroom, Aimee and her classmates worked in groups to develop age-appropriate games that helped break negative stereotypes for the kids. They wanted to make learning fun by having each game encourage conversation by including depictions that highlighted positive possibilities for all people. The students shared the three game prototypes with Kathy and Nathan and then made changes. Next the students visited with the children and played the new games together. After that visit, the games were fine-tuned into the final versions that were graded using preestablished criteria they'd been given at the beginning of the semester.

Throughout this service-learning project, the college students kept reflection journals, writing in response to prompts Dr. Thomas had provided. They described expectations before going into the community as well as impressions after Kathy and Nathan's visit to class. They wrote again after the "get acquainted" trip. They also noted what they learned concerning children's perceptions of media, the course subject matter, how the games worked (or did not), and how they could impact the lives of children positively in the future.

At the end of the semester, Dr. Thomas invited Kathy and Nathan back. They talked about what the children said about the games and offered their own ideas. Everybody agreed the service-learning project gave the college students greater understanding of how media could influence children. They all noted that games could help the kids think more critically about media and agreed that this was pretty important. Kathy and Nathan took the final versions of the games back with them and encouraged the students to stay involved with the children and the club.

As you can see, an academic service-learning course provides more than classroom instruction. The Media and Culture students extended their learning by working with kids in the community. The actual learning happened as they reflected in writing and through class discussions about the children, the subject matter, and their future contributions to their communities. Reflection is the hallmark of academic service-learning and one important way it's distinct from volunteering.

Still, sometimes extended volunteering can follow a service-learning class. Aimee and Sabrina were so inspired by the service-learning project that they contacted Kathy to see if they could do more. Working collaboratively, the three conceived of having teens at the center write and act in plays about media that would then be filmed and preserved.

This complex project gave the teenagers new experiences, used Aimee's and Sabrina's skills in media production, and produced a video that the children (and teens) could watch over and over again. In the process, the teens made important contributions: sharing ways to make the videos relevant to the kids, helping write scripts, serving as actors and narrators, and also choosing scenes in the community where video footage would be filmed.

Aimee and Sabrina repeatedly went back to the teens and to Kathy to make sure they were making the best possible video. They learned a lot over those last two years they were in college. Kathy and the teens even held a celebration with children, their parents, and other members of the club's community to view the final video. Everyone thanked Aimee and Sabrina for their hard work and encouraged them to share the video as they looked for first jobs after college.

A different type of community engagement involves community-engaged research jointly planned and carried out by campus and community members. Think back to the example from chapter 1 about how Becca's research team worked in full partnership with Shena and parents to develop new puppetry scripts about healthy eating for children. They had also collected data from focus groups (after getting approval from the university and consent from the parents); Becca's team including Shena shared their work with the puppetry at conferences and through scholarly publications (see Thomson, Dumlao, & Howard, 2016, for a related example). In addition, Becca worked more with Shena to write two newsletter articles to share with parents and others in the community.

Yet another variation of community engagement is sustained volunteerism between one community organization and a student group/organization. For example, the Baseball for All program leader came to the campus service-learning center to find out whether college students could help some special needs kids play baseball on Saturdays. Nichelle, the assistant director, connected the Student Life Club with the baseball organization, and every Saturday at least five students went to the ball field.

By the following summer, some of these college students were serving as trusted mentors when "their kids" participated in Special Olympics games nearby. After that, the Student Life Club worked with the kids, their parents, and staff at the ballpark every year; the connections ran deep!

Community-Campus Partners Rely on Interpersonal Communication

No matter which type of community engagement is involved, partners rely on communication to share information and to achieve other tasks together. Because we can't read others' minds or know what others are thinking, communication is essential. This communication is more than mere talk or sending messages back and forth, though. "People do not simply send meaning from one to the other and then back again; rather, they build shared meaning . . . through *simultaneous* sending and receiving" (West & Turner, 2006, p. 17). Predominant scholarly thinking about human interpersonal communication uses the transactional model of communication (National Communication Association, 2016; see also Barnlund, 1970; Watzlawick, Beavin, & Jackson, 1967) as shown in Figure 2.1.

Figure 2.1. Transactional model of communication.

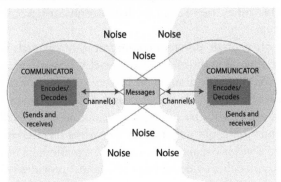

The Transactional Model of Communication and How It Works

Partnership communication is complex and allows for rich meaning-making. But partnership communication can also create misunderstandings at various points in the process so it's important to understand how the multi-directional transactional model of communication works.

Each communicator in an interaction encodes thoughts and feelings into verbal and nonverbal messages. Sometimes encoding is thoughtful and planned. But sometimes encoding is automatic, without careful thought, and we hear someone say, "I just said that without thinking!"

Each communicator also decodes verbal and nonverbal messages received. The message itself has no inherent meaning. Instead, the individual makes sense of incoming data by processing the information using well-established mental patterns that reflect cultural as well as personal values, characteristics, and experiences.

Consider the example of Juanita, who volunteered every Saturday at the literacy center and so regularly interacted with Toni, the organization's leader. One day as Juanita was talking, she noticed Toni's animated facial expressions. At first, Juanita thought Toni was in a hurry and wanted her to leave. But then Juanita stopped herself to ask questions about what those facial expressions actually meant. She spoke out, explaining, "Toni, I notice that your face is very animated. I'm not sure what the expressions I am seeing really mean. Can you tell me?"

Toni laughed. Turns out Toni was excited to have Juanita take a sincere interest in the clients and could see the impact this work was making on their daily lives. But until Juanita asked her about it, Toni didn't even realize that her facial expressions reflected her excitement.

Both partners recognized that messages between them could follow different pathways or what communication experts call *channels*. For instance, face-to-face communication uses a different channel than media communication. As their partnership developed, Toni and Juanita met some-times, but other times used e-mail to share details for upcoming volunteer work.

Interestingly enough, different communication channels have different qualities, including amount of feedback, level of immediacy, the kinds of raw data received, and the amount of privacy offered. For example, think about the last time you got a text message that didn't make sense. There were no facial expressions, no tone of voice, and no other feedback to help you understand. You could only rely on the words themselves. In contrast, when you use a video-enhanced channel like Facetime or Skype, you get more nonverbal details. A video-enhanced channel provides richer raw data and is usually immediate, without the delay of typing that happens with a text message.

Choosing among channels for messages can be crucial. Some channels work better for a select purpose. People also have preferences for channels. Think back to the interactions between Rachel and Shannon in chapter 1. Those partners had to decide whether the best channel for their first meet-ing would be face-to-face conversations, Skype interactions, or a phone call. They also recognized after the phone call that they had distinct preferences for specific communication channels, as shown in Table 2.1.

Another aspect of communication is called *noise*. Anything that interferes with a message being shared is considered noise. For instance, a communicator might not be fully involved in conversation because of the physiological noise created by hunger when talking close to lunchtime. Another communicator might not be able to think clearly and absorb information due to the noise created in a room that is way too hot. Of course, noise in the traditional sense can impact interactions, too. Communicators could be startled by a slammed door and totally lose track of what they were talking about. Eliminating or reducing unwanted noise is a great practice to provide a good space for part-ners to communicate.

For example, Ramon, the president of the campus leadership organiza-tion, wanted to talk to Dennis, the director of the civic engagement center, right away about their upcoming alternative break trip. The only time Dennis could meet that day was just before lunch. But the whole time they talked, both Dennis and Ramon found it difficult to listen to what the other had to say. Thankfully, they both recognized that hunger-related noise was getting in the way of their normally productive conversations. So they decided to set another meeting two days later to work out details for the trip; both hurried off to get their lunches. (Of course, had they known about this in advance, they could have had a "working lunch" meeting.) Their change in plans was,

TABLE 2.1

Qualities of Different Communication Channels or Tools

Channel/Tool	Immediate Availability	Delay Time	Communication Features	Collaborative Communication Framework Uses	Benefits	Limits
Face-to-face	Yes	No	Verbal and multiple nonverbal cues	Connecting Conversing Committing (some ways) Envisioning Partner patterns	Share content as well as relational and identity information between partners	Possibility that other commitments or time differences can make scheduling tough
Phone	Yes	Yes, voice message	Verbal, voice tone, energy level, no other nonverbals	Connecting Conversing Sometimes partner patterns	Useful way to contact if both available	Limited nonverbal info Phone not always answered so there could be delay in receipt of voice message
E-mail	Yes	Yes	Written, sometimes with visuals	Connecting Sharing about other framework elements	Good for documents "Paper" trail	No nonverbals or relational, identity messages

(Continues)

Table 2.1. (*Continued*)

Channel/ Tool	Immediate Availability	Delay Time	Communication Features	Collaborative Communication Framework Uses	Benefits	Limits
Text Messages	Yes	Yes, possibly	Written, some visuals	Connecting Conversing Envisioning Could be partner patterns	Message with one or more Mobilize people on-the-ground efforts Share visuals or short videos	No nonverbals or relational, identity messages Relies on WiFi or phone access
GroupMe	Yes	Yes, possibly	Written, some visuals	Connecting Conversing somewhat Envisioning Could be partner patterns	Group free messaging with phone app or SMS Mobilize on-the-ground efforts Visuals or short videos	No nonverbals or relational, identity messages Relies on WiFi or phone access
Facetime, Skype, or Google Voice and Google Hangout	Yes	No	Audio and visual; chat functions	Connecting Conversing Envisioning Partner patterns	Can connect one or more across distances; both visual and auditory	Requires computer or app access Need account Cost for some services with Skype or Google Voice
One Drive	No	Yes	Written and visual, linked to other Microsoft products	Connecting Sharing related to other collaborative communication elements	Cloud-based documents or visuals, slides Collaborative work	Requires computer or app access as well as an account Comes preinstalled on Windows 10

Google Docs	Yes, can edit in real time	Yes	Written and visual, can convert some other documents	Connecting Collaborating on a document Sharing related to other collaborative communication elements	Cloud-based documents or visuals, slides Collaborative work	Requires computer or app access as well as an account
Facebook	Yes	Yes	Written, videos, visuals, linked to other media	Connecting Share information regarding other framework elements	Useful for distribution to some key networks via Facebook group page Facebook Messenger offers texts with individuals and groups	Limited privacy in general, but can be set for greater privacy.
Twitter	Yes	Yes	Send short messages	Connecting Quick updates	Wide audience Hashtags align topics Spread ideas—potentially quickly	One-way Short messages, no context

Note. Partners can use this table (and expand on it with others) to determine how they will communicate for different purposes and in varied contexts.

GroupMe (see www.groupme.com) and Microsoft's One Drive (see www.onedrive.live.com) are newer tools that many students use effectively when communicating with one another in an online group communication class.

though, a great way to manage unwanted noise and to have both partners able to fully concentrate on their conversation.

Interestingly enough, each communicator brings his or her past into current communication through his or her unique fields of experience. Simply put, a field of experience is the accumulation of an individual's values, attitudes, and beliefs derived from cultural, personal, and other experiences. One's field of experience greatly influences the communication process; it's more than just mere reference points. A field of experience impacts the way a person understands the message as well as what factors matter to that person as he or she communicates.

Think about this: Samora had been in North Carolina for nearly six months but still didn't feel at home. She'd come back with her new American husband, Dean, after his military assignment in Okinawa ended. They'd met during Dean's deployment, fallen in love, and married after just a year. They'd been really happy in Okinawa even though they had little alone time. Samora was used to that, even though Dean was not. In her experience, there were always other people around; she was rarely alone.

But now in the United States, she found herself isolated every time Dean went off to work. He seemed to like working independently. But it was confusing to her. She didn't know what to say to Dean and became increasingly quiet when he was home. One night Dean told her that he'd noticed she seemed unhappy and different than before. They talked about it. Then he began to understand.

The very next day, Dean took Samora along to the base so she could visit with other military wives at the Good Neighbor Center. The center director, Anne, asked Samora to help plan a party for other newcomers. Samora was thrilled and excitedly told Anne that she was really good at preparing bento boxes. Anne loved that idea and put Samara in charge of party food. A week later, they went together to the stores to get supplies. The other wives enthusiastically helped prepare the Bento boxes, too.

At the party, Samora had more fun than she'd had in a long, long time. Everybody loved the Bento boxes and it felt really good to be part of a community again. Dean loved seeing Samora light up and noticed her talking to many people. It had been a long time since he'd seen her so animated.

Dean learned something important then: Being independent was a totally different way of life for Samora—it was not part of her field of experience and confused her, making her quieter. But now that he knew this, Dean could help her find ways to regularly interact with people both on and off base and create the community she needed. It worked! Samora began to talk about loving her new home. Also, she gradually learned to be content spending a little more time alone.

In sum, then, our field of experience impacts communication in multiple ways. It not only acts as a filter for what information gets attention but also impacts how each of us processes the incoming information we receive and, subsequently, the way we communicate with others.

The Word *Transactional* Has Different Meanings

The transactional model of communication is the basis for the ways that communication can be used in *any* partnership—whether in the workplace or another setting—to create understanding between people. Consequently, this model (and the use of the word *transactional* in the model's name) is important to community-based work. But the word *transactional* has other meanings in the community engagement literature, so it's important to sort this out.

Enos and Morton (2003), for instance, compared transactional relationships to transformative relationships, a conceptualization further developed by Clayton, Bringle, Senor, Huq, and Morrison (2010). These ideas definitely help us understand the nature, intent, and possibilities of different kinds of community-engaged partnerships.

Transactional relationships are designed to complete a task and work within existing structures rather than to promote dramatic change within the partners or the partnership (Enos & Morton, 2003, p. 24). Transformative relationships, in contrast, engage partners in ways that transcend short-term goals to create larger meaning and potentially impact communities in innovative ways (pp. 24–25). Thus, transformative relationships expect partners to change and grow as part of both the relationship and their joint work.

Importantly, though, the model of transactional communication, as defined by contemporary communication scholars, would apply to *both* transactional and transformative relationships. This communication model represents "the collaborative and ongoing message exchange between individuals, or an individual and a group of individuals, with the goal of understanding each other" (National Communication Association, 2016). That is, *this model explains human communication across settings with varied purposes or intentions but with the overarching goal of building shared understanding.* Thus, the elements found in this model can help us understand key communication processes so we can build different kinds of partnerships to meet our purposes within the community—including both the transformational and transformative ones described earlier.

Partnerships and Relational Communication

When community engagement partners work together collaboratively, their communication, by definition, is relationally based and ongoing. Galvin and Wilkinson (2006) note that relational communication is a "dynamic and continuous process. Each relationship develops its own communication history, a history that cannot be rewritten" (p. 5) no matter what happens later on.

One useful visual that captures the continuousness of communication in a relationship is a spiral or helix (see Figure 2.2). Imagine this spiral shaped so that communication, as represented by a line, can be less frequent, creating a wider distance between partners (i.e., wider circles) or more frequent with a smaller distance between partners (i.e., narrower circles). Notably, the line representing the communication stream between partners continues as long as the relationship endures (see also a model of relational communication by Galvin & Wilkinson, 2006, p. 6).

Notably, partner communication is influenced by internal factors (e.g., the partners and the partnership characteristics) as well as external factors (e.g., the organizations represented and the larger world). That is, relational communication is embedded or nested within multiple contexts that can impact partner interactions (see also ideas by Bronfenbrenner, 2009).

Figure 2.2. Communication spiral in partnerships.

Line = communication stream between partners

Width of the spiral = frequency of communication

Beginning of Partnership

Key Principles of Partnership Communication

Many guidelines are offered for effective partnerships in general (e.g., see Holland, 2005), but less attention has been given to communication specifically. Effective communication between community-campus partners can follow several key principles of interpersonal communication identified by Wood (2007).

Principle 1: We Cannot Not Communicate

When we are with others, we are communicating something even when we are silent. That is, when we don't talk, our partner is likely to make assumptions about why we are being silent. Our partner may also look at our facial expressions or posture and draw conclusions.

In some cultures, silence is a way to indicate respect and careful listening. But there are other possible understandings of silence. Your partner could feel that he or she was being ignored if you didn't say a thing despite sitting nearby. Any time we are with others we are sending messages even when we don't communicate intentionally or verbally.

Principle 2: Interpersonal Communication Is Irreversible

Whatever we say can't be erased or reversed. There's no way to retract spoken words; anyone who hears our words will have a memory of that interaction, and there are records of interpersonal communication through many other channels as well. If we use e-mail, for instance, there is a record. You may have noticed stories on the news about hackers getting hold of messages shared through e-mails. (One professor actually told students to think about an e-mail like a postcard that can be read by many, not just by the intended reader. This idea is important to keep in mind when using e-mail or social media.)

Principle 3: Interpersonal Communication Involves Ethical Choices

As we communicate with one another, we choose how we will treat others. We can be fair and just—or not! As you will learn throughout this book, best practices for community engagement involve making ethical decisions about the levels of reciprocity, mutual benefit, shared vision, shared purpose, and so on. (More to come about these concepts later in the book.)

Principle 4: People Construct Meanings Through Communication

No meaning exists inherently in words or other symbols that we might share with one another. Instead, the transactional model of communication assumes that people encode and decode the raw material and use their own field of experience to make sense of it. Meaning-making or sense-making done face-to-face is complex but even more so when it comes to modern-day technology used by partners.

For instance, many media sources of information use one-way transmission of information from a sender to receiver(s) rather than the multidirectional process involved in interpersonal communication. Television is a good example of one-way transmission of ideas (a packaged set of messages) that are interpreted or decoded by viewers/listeners using their unique field of experience. Two partners listening to the same media message are quite likely to come away with different understandings of what they saw and heard, depending on their field of experience and the cultural and other filters that help them pay attention to different elements of the message.

Some social media or text-messaging channels are immediate, with senders and receivers interacting simultaneously in real time—such as communicating through Skype with video or Facetime. In this instance, partners also interpret the message using the field of experience, but like face-to-face interactions, there is a multidirectional flow of information—including nonverbal information that is exchanged between the two partners involved in the communication.

No matter what communication channel partners choose, meaning-making is not automatic. Rather, incoming information has to be interpreted and understood regardless of how it comes to us, so we continue to construct meanings over time as we communicate with our partners. Building shared meaning is an ongoing process!

Principle 5: Metacommunication Affects Meanings

Metacommunication simply means communicating about communication. Sometimes, letting people know the intent behind a message, either verbal or nonverbal, can change the receiver's understanding of that message.

Consider a time when you might have said something in anger to a friend, without thinking it through. Your friend might have reacted with stunned disbelief because the words were out of character for you. But later, when you talked about specifics (i.e., metacommunicated), your partner may have recognized that there were outside circumstances that contributed to your use of the angry words. The friend may be willing to forgive and set aside what was seen and heard that one time due to knowing it wasn't really "who you are" together. (This is why having a generally positive communication climate really matters.) Metacommunication can modify the partner's reaction after that initial exchange. Metacommunication can also bring out latent, under-the-surface, and unrecognized information that the partners can use as they continue to interact.

Understanding nonverbal communication with our partner often involves metacommunication. We can talk about our gestures, tone of voice, movement, and so on to clarify meaning or to establish common understandings with our partner.

Think back to the example of Juanita checking about Toni's facial expression earlier in the chapter. The questions she asked Toni served as metacommunication, communication about communication. She asked questions to learn more about the meaning behind those nonverbal facial expressions she observed. (Find more about this topic in chapter 4.) Metacommunication is an important way to build deeper understanding between people.

Principle 6: Interpersonal Communication Develops and Sustains Relationships

When we meet someone for the first time, we may know little to nothing about that person. It's through communication that we learn about this person and identify both commonalities and differences. As the relationship develops, a person can share or disclose less obvious information so we get a deeper understanding of who that individual really is. Think back to the story of Shrek and the layers that people have, as explained in chapter 1. It's through communication that we bring out the information from those deeper layers and share it with one another.

Further, through communication with our partners we work out our expectations of one another as well as what exactly we will do together. Over time, relationships take on unique meanings through a history of communication between partners and their joint work as illustrated by the communication spiral in partnerships presented in Figure 2.2. This history of communication in a relationship is also how we develop a sense of the relational climate and the relational culture discussed in chapter 1.

Principle 7: Interpersonal Communication Is Not a Panacea

There's no one right way to communicate in any particular situation or with any specific person. It's just not possible to predict exactly what will happen when we communicate, even when we have the best of intentions. Messiness happens!

Differences between people come out when we talk; sometimes these differences can't be easily resolved. Still it's important to address differences that are causing ongoing or intense reactions between partners. People sometimes need to agree to disagree, hopefully with civility and respect. Or they may need to come up with other ways to manage their relationship to continue working well together. So, although important, communication can't fix everything. Still, communication can help us build shared meanings and solve many of the problems we face—together.

Principle 8: Interpersonal Communication Effectiveness Can Be Learned

Each of us has the opportunity to learn more about communication all across our lives. It's not a one and done kind of learning. We need, for instance, to continue to learn about ways to use still-developing communication technology such as social media to more effectively build and sustain relationships. We also need to continue learning about our partner and how we can work better together.

Competent communication choices depend on the people involved, the context, the channel, and more. In this book, the focus is on building a repertoire of collaborative communication knowledge and practices to serve as a foundation for choice-making. Learning to understand and use the eight principles just described can build a solid base for an ever-expanding collaborative communication repertoire.

Communication and Partnership Ideals

The community engagement literature outlines partnership ideals like reciprocity, mutual benefit, shared power, sustainable relationships, and so on. These partnership ideals both *impact* and *reflect* communication processes and practices. Indeed, human communication is what brings these ideals or values to life. So, "how" communication between partners happens matters—a lot!

For example, the ideas of *reciprocity* or *mutual benefit* strongly implicate choosing communication styles and practices where all partner voices will be heard fully. Stoecker and Tryon (2009), as well as Sandy and Holland (2006), have pointed out that community partner voices need to be included in all aspects of partnership work, from start to finish.

Think back to the introductory story about the student interested in developing a playground for children. To be more "reciprocal" and create "mutual benefit," collaborative conversations with both campus and community members actively involved were required throughout the process of planning and building the playground and contributed to ownership of the park.

Another partnership ideal, *shared power*, often necessitates putting communication processes or rules into place so that different partners have a say or have other forms of power when decisions are being made or when results are being shared. (Developing shared power frequently involves metacommunication, involving talk about communication processes or rules that may not all be obvious to all until shared.)

Sometimes expectations for communication can be detailed formally such as through a memorandum of understanding (MOU) between the university and the community organization partnering. But expectations and guidelines for interactions can also be informal or even implied between two people. This happens when partners identify ways that they want to contribute to the ongoing work equally or equitably. (An example of this was shared in chapter 1 when Sarah wanted to be a co-educator with Dr. Aaron as they worked equitably with college students to address needs at the animal shelter.) Building and maintaining shared power is a process that can be revisited over time through communication.

Overall, communication is key to enacting the partnership ideals that make up best practices for community engagement, no matter what form we are using. In service-learning, for instance, students have the opportunity to learn more about developing equitable, mutually beneficial partnerships as they simultaneously learn new ways to build a communication repertoire. In community-engaged scholarship, the community members and research team members also have an opportunity to enact *best practices of community engagement* or partnership ideals as they interact both interpersonally and through various forms of media.

In sum, complex, competent communication is essential for building an effective, sustainable partnership. Learning about collaborative communication practices and processes is therefore not just nice but absolutely necessary to accomplish the positive change we want to see as we work together in our communities.

But this goes beyond just our community engagement work. What you learn about collaborative communication can be applied to other relationships as well. The knowledge and skills in this book are transferrable to many settings, when working with many different kinds of people. So, read on.

Putting Chapter Ideas Into Action

Action for Partnerships and Teaching About Partnerships

1. Think back to different times you've experienced a sense of success in your current partnership. What was it like? What do you think made it successful or fulfilling? Now share your thoughts with your partner(s).

Were your ideas similar or different? Use this information to have a discussion about the partnership and what you might want to do to foster more successes in the future.

2. Using Table 2.2, write notes in the margins or on a separate paper about how you might build those different ideals in your current partnership. To make this fun, you might draw a picture of the current state of the partnership. Encourage your partner to do the same thing. Then compare your pictures. Ask what these pictures show you about your relationship. Can you improve it? If so, how?

Action for Community-Engaged Scholarship

1. Barbara Holland (2005) asserts that we know a great deal about partnership characteristics but have much less scholarly knowledge about how to make partnerships work, particularly in light of power differences, race/cultural issues, language differences, leadership practices, and so on (pp. 15–16). Consider these ideas in light of your own area of expertise and your current community-engaged scholarship. What action steps can you put in place to move forward to learn more about partnership practices and making them work better? What can you do to move the scholarship forward by collaborating with your academic or community colleagues representing other disciplines or organizations?

2. Characterize, in one or two sentences, your own approach to community-engaged scholarship. That is, how would you explain the community-engaged scholarship you do to someone who doesn't know a thing about it? Once you've written this down, get feedback from others outside your area of expertise or discipline about how they understood your characterization. Did they understand it the way you thought they would? Would some changes in your writing (and subsequent speaking) help convey your intended meaning more effectively? You can develop an elevator speech or short summary of what you do to share in an instant. This practice can help you spread the word about community-engaged work quickly. It can also help others know about the important scholarly work you are doing and why it matters!

Important Note: This last activity could be used when preparing to share your community-engaged scholarship through journals or conferences (especially when multiple disciplines or perspectives are represented). You could also share your characterization with your community partner(s) in order to get usable feedback and/or to build your shared understandings about the work

TABLE 2.2
Communication and Community-Engaged Partnership Ideals

Community Engagement Partnership Ideal	Communication Needed	Suggestions to Applications
Reciprocity	Requires channel or tool that allows for simultaneous two-way communication *or* back-and-forth communication without long delays	Relates to all aspects of the collaborative communication framework; requires ongoing work between partners
Mutual Benefit	Needs to have involvement by partners in communication that incorporates multiple views and perspectives; requires conversing about what partners need, want, expect, and so on	Relates to all aspects of the collaborative communication framework; requires ongoing work between partners
Shared Power	Requires awareness that power can be conveyed verbally and nonverbally—sometimes in subtle ways; work to equalize power between partners in both ways	Recognition that conversations about how best to share power given partner's respective organizational responsibilities and expectations are important
Trust	Happens through verbal communication and actions; can be fragile, especially with newer partnerships between diverse groups	Focus on trust-building conversations and actions, using metacommunication to learn what matters to the other partner(s)
Ethical Considerations	Recognizes that community engagement ethics may be distinct in some ways from other ethical considerations in teaching and scholarship	Awareness that all of the other partnership ideals have ethical components to be considered in ongoing partner communication; also directly impacted at partner level by what happens at other levels of organizations involved
Sustainable Relationships	Understands that conversing about the relationship as well as the tasks matters	Focus on long-term relationships rather than just on short-term goals when communicating with partners; understanding that sometimes relational repair will be needed; and keeping in mind milestones previously met and the hopefully positive relationship to date can help

you are doing together. Further, if you want to use your community-engaged scholarship in promotion and tenure processes, it's important to gather data about why the scholarship matters not only to you but also to others in the community. Your characterization of your work in writing and through your speaking is an important first step toward explaining not just why you do this scholarship but why it matters to the university, to the community, and beyond!

3

THE COLLABORATIVE COMMUNICATION FRAMEWORK

One good conversation won't be enough. Strong relationships require nurturing, flexible communication over time.

—Rebecca J. Dumlao

To be collaborative, interpersonal communication must be grounded in a partnership mind-set. Such a mind-set allows us to consistently juggle our thoughts to include multiple perspectives at once. As Kare Anderson (2014b) points out, a mutuality mind-set can enable people to "speak sooner to the strongest sweet spot of shared interest."

This book focuses specifically on collaborative communication that helps build and sustain community-campus partnerships. As used here, *collaborative communication is the set of communication practices that promote a relational perspective, showing respect and openness to the partner along with his or her unique contributions and views. With collaborative collaboration, new possibilities can be created for the partnership itself and for partners' joint work in the community.*

The thinking that undergirds collaborative communication includes attention to the partnership (the "we") as well as attention to the individual partner's needs and concerns (the "me") to reach beyond both.

Phillips and Wood (1983) use the term *dual perspective* for attending to and understanding our own and our partner's perspectives, beliefs, thoughts, or feelings. This complex, multifocused thinking involves managing one's own concerns enough to learn about the other person's concerns. Dual-perspective thinking can allow us to be flexible and adaptable enough to take in new incoming information about the partner through mindful listening and then to shape our subsequent communication and actions toward mutuality.

Mindful Listening: Openness to the Partner

Mindful listening is more than just the physical act of hearing the sound waves that touch our ears. Mindful listening also goes beyond what Ting-Toomey and Chung (2012) call "mindless listening" (p. 200). Those using mindless listening hear selectively, prioritizing their own positions and concerns so only some information gets in. Mindless listeners only take in information that supports their own assumptions, positions, and concerns; what doesn't support their views is screened out. Unfortunately, this mindless listening creates a serious barrier to working well together.

In contrast, mindful listening involves openness to incoming information—including being present to receive unspoken or nonverbal cues. Ting-Toomey and Chung (2012) point out that "*ting* (the Chinese word for listening) means 'attending mindfully with our ears, eyes, and a focused heart,' to the sounds, tone, gestures, movements, nonverbal nuances, pauses, and silence" (p. 199) that we witness. This kind of mindful listening provides more data for partners to use.

Also, when using mindful listening, interpretations can be subject to change if incoming verbal or nonverbal communication alters what we first understood. Mindful listening then offers the flexibility to develop a deeper, holistic understanding between partners that can lead toward innovation or change as we work together. (More specifics about listening follow in chapter 4.)

Going Beyond Tolerance to Respect

All too often, we focus on accepting the other in a casual way, simply tolerating the differences between us, and think that's enough. Tolerance is better than hostility or indifference or ego-centeredness, to be sure. But tolerance is not receptive enough to gather the rich details that true partnerships require.

A deeper sense of respect and even admiration can be achieved when we choose to learn more about the other person's perspectives and then become full partners. This doesn't mean that we agree with everything the partner thinks, says, or does, but it does mean that we are open to each other. To echo Kare Anderson once more, mutuality matters in a connected era. We need to find a shared interest more quickly than ever before in order to do something better together (Anderson, 2014a).

Collaborative Communication Framework: Choices for Partners

The collaborative communication framework provides a starting point for partners to make communication choices as they navigate their ongoing relationship. Five elements constitute the framework: connect, converse, envision, commit, and partner patterns. These five are all necessary to foster the highest quality partnership interactions and promote distinctive results for the communities involved.

There are many ways we can "do" collaborative communication using the elements in the framework. There is no one set formula. Contacts usually start with connection and conversation and proceed with envisioning and committing before developing unique partner patterns. But once we are working together, the elements in the collaborative communication framework can be navigated in any direction. Each partner can pick and choose among the framework elements as circumstances and needs require.

Even so, all elements of the collaborative communication framework are needed for us as partners to facilitate individual and/or community transformation (see Figure 3.1). That's because these communication elements align with well-recognized best practices for effective community-campus partnerships: reciprocity, mutual benefit, ethical behavior, cultural sensitivity, and shared power, among others. Through collaborative communication, partners can foster a relationship that supports them in creating new realities for their community(ies).

Figure 3.1. Collaborative communication framework.

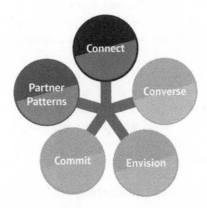

Looking Deeper at the Elements: Connecting

Connecting involves communication to find common ground and establish rapport and closeness in the relationship with our partner. Connecting can happen through verbal communication, nonverbal communication, or a combination of the two.

Deep connecting tends to infuse energy and passion to create positive emotion; it involves the heart and the soul, not just the mind. Thus, deep connecting uses both emotional and social intelligences (Goleman, 2007) to promote relational closeness and interdependence so we can share what matters with the other (see Guerrero, Anderson, & Afifi, 2018, p. 170). Connecting, in this sense, *is* what bonds community-engaged partners, making us more than two people casually communicating or even two people working together on a short-term project.

Competent connecting can, for instance, focus on how each partner most readily receives and understands information. That is, individual learning styles predispose individuals to process incoming information in patterned ways to quickly make meaning (see Gardner, 2006; Kress, 2010; Markova & MacArthur, 2015). For visual learners, it may be important to see the partner. For auditory learners, the imperative is to hear the partner. Linguistic learners need to see or hear the words. Still others may prefer to touch or be physically near the other to process information kinesthetically. Some learners require varied types of incoming information to understand fully.

Navigating differences in connecting may require partners to use detective work, including observation and questioning (i.e., metacommunication), to identify the best ways to communicate. A common mistake is to assume that the other person connects in the same way(s) we do. For better results, partners can discuss what helps each one feel deeply connected and listen mindfully. Or each partner can carefully observe what is happening communicatively when he or she gets enthusiastic or insightful responses from the other. Once gathered, we can mentally store this information to use later as connecting shorthand—quick ways to connect with our partner—when that is needed.

In sum, think about connecting as a "home base" where partners rebond with one another. Letting go of outside influences to connect and be present with the partner proves especially important when resolving any differences that come up. When we connect well, we offer information that matters to our partner and show that we care about him or her and the relationship, not just on the work we do together.

Take-Away Lessons About Connecting

- Connecting happens more readily when we focus on the needs of the partner and the partnership (not on self).
- Mindful listening means being fully present, observing and listening carefully to the partner rather than trying to multitask.
- Connecting serves as the relational glue that can help partners stay bonded, even when difficulties arise.

Looking Deeper at the Elements: Conversing

Conversing involves interactive dialogue that goes back and forth between partners to create understanding by sharing information or exploring ideas. Conversing involves transferring information, clarifying positions, or even talking through differences of opinion or perspective. Conversing is where the day-to-day collaborative communication work happens.

Conversations rely heavily on verbal information, on the content being shared, to develop meanings between people. Mindful listening matters a great deal as we seek to understand one another. (See chapter 4 for more on listening.)

However, nonverbal information can modify, supplement, or even contradict verbal information. Nonverbal information can include body movements like facial expressions and eye contact, vocal characteristics like pitch or loudness, touch, physical distance between people, use of time, physical appearance including possessions, and information from the surroundings (McCornack, 2013, p. 218). Interestingly enough, nonverbal information helps signify who we are, demonstrates our feelings, and can offer other relational information that's vital in a partnership.

Wood (2007) details three dimensions of relationship-level meanings: responsiveness, liking, and power. Responsiveness is often demonstrated through eye contact, facial expressions, and body posture that show our interest in relating to the other (p. 136). "Nonverbal behaviors often are keen indicators of how positively or negatively we feel toward others" (p. 136), how much we like them. Facial expressions like smiles, gentle touches, or even open arms can all indicate liking. Tuning in to this important information can help create a positive relational climate between partners.

Power can be asserted through space, touch, and time (pp. 136–137). For instance, the large corner office is typically reserved for a supervisor, whereas staff members are housed in cubicles. Also, a person with greater power is more likely to touch someone with lower power than the other way around. In addition, someone with recognized importance, such as a doctor, can make the partner (e.g., patient) wait. Power can be exerted nonverbally in multiple ways.

Major cultural differences exist for nonverbal signals, too. Ting-Toomey and Chung (2012) point out that "the same nonverbal signal can mean different things to different people in different cultures. For example, the 'OK' sign in the United States can mean the number zero in France, can mean '$' in Japan, and can be interpreted as an obscene gesture in Spain" (p. 134).

Despite popular press to the contrary, it's important to recognize that body language and other nonverbals don't have set meanings. So whenever you draw a conclusion about what a nonverbal behavior means, it's wise to hold that conclusion tentatively until you gather more details to confirm or disconfirm your initial judgment. Also, experts say people tend to rely more heavily on a nonverbal message than the verbal one when the two clash. So learning about nonverbal communication can be a very important capacity when working in community-campus partnerships.

In sum, nonverbal cues are critical in defining relational meanings. Over time, they influence the relational "tone" and help develop the overall relational climate. Nonverbal messages, used well, can help create a positively oriented partnership with a mutuality mind-set. Partners can use verbal and nonverbal information through conversations to enable them to work better together.

Take-Away Lessons About Conversing

- Conversing is the only way to learn what the other person is really thinking and feeling, because we can't read minds.
- Even with our best intentions, conversations can get messy.
- Talking shares information. Mindful listening and receiving partner feedback promotes shared understanding.
- Nonverbal cues can speak louder than words because they are more likely to be believed.

Looking Deeper at the Elements: Envisioning

Envisioning involves dreaming about what's possible for a community and crystallizing those possibilities in communication between and among the partners. Envisioning often starts by verbally expressing bold possibilities without having every detail in place. Envisioning can involve drawings or other symbolic representations of what the future might look like. Later, partners define specifics in targeted, doable actions. Specifics can be communicated through time lines, flowcharts, design renderings, or logic models, as well as through written plans.

Multiple people representing the campus and community may do the initial large-scale envisioning work. Many different capabilities will be needed—for instance, generating solutions for large issues or highly complex, wicked problems that can't be solved readily.

Envisioning also happens, though, on day-to-day matters between two partners working together to carry out a larger vision. At times, these partners may want to revisit the big-picture vision to share with supporters or the public to get "buy-in" and commitment to the vision. This sharing can involve both interpersonal communication and media channels that reach and meet the sensory preferences and needs of the contributors or community stakeholders.

Envisioning processes involve complex thinking, drilling down from abstract ideas to detail specific action steps and back again—often more than once. Two different kinds of thinking—fluid intelligence and crystalline intelligence (along with related communication)—help accomplish this.

Potter (2014) defines *fluid intelligence* as "the ability to be creative, make leaps of insight, and perceive things in a fresh and novel matter" by taking a new view and then working backward "to construct a logical path between the new position and the (innovative, intuitive, or creative) starting point" (p. 88).

In contrast, *crystalline intelligence* means taking in a large set of symbolic data and their meanings, compiling information. "Highly developed crystalline intelligence gives us the facility to absorb the images, definitions, opinions, and agendas of others" (p. 88) through systematic, logical thinking.

Both cognitive abilities, to be creative as well as to form logical systems or steps, are necessary for envisioning work. During idea generation, communication practices and methods of sharing need to be flexible, to allow for playing with ideas. Imagine drawing on a whiteboard or using design templates or brainstorming cards as the creative possibilities flow. Such communication could be more "old school" using established methods or more innovative using social media tools to gather and share information about the big picture.

Later, when developing the logical action steps that lead toward implementation, linear step-by-step communication practices are likely. Approaches like flowcharts or logic models or even an elaborated timeline can facilitate changes and help partners stay accountable for accomplishing the needed steps or stages.

Envisioning necessitates flexibility, as well as risk-taking or creative courage, and is built on trust and communication between partners. Things will change and unexpected challenges will arise. To deal with these situations, both the dyadic partners and the larger team will need to communicate often and well in order to bring the desired possibilities to life.

Take-Away Lessons About Envisioning

- Envisioning communication moves an abstract vision toward specific actions to bring dreams to life.
- People may have well-established capacities with creativity or logical thinking; envisioning requires both!

- Communicating our vision by engaging multiple senses and communication channels is more likely to create shared meaning for more stakeholders (or contributors).

Looking Deeper at the Elements: Committing

Committing refers to reaching agreements about responsibilities, roles, relationship specifics, and ways the partnership will work. Such agreements happen through communicating at multiple levels—between partners, organizations, and the communities they serve.

At the dyadic level, nurturing the partner and building the partnership involves a commitment *to the other person.* Ideally, we want to trust and respect our partner fully and know that he or she will care and support us while we work together.

Detailing an interpersonal or partnership-level commitment can reinforce shared understandings built through connecting and conversing. Words like "I promise to be there for you when you need me" are important to say verbally.

But the promise of commitment can be implied and demonstrated by actions as well. Sometimes actions do speak louder than words! For example, imagine how you would react if your partner turned his back to you while saying that he was committed to working with you. This contrast between the nonverbal posturing and the words would make it hard to believe what he said. Instead, if he leaned toward you when saying he promised to be there if you needed him, you would see greater consistency between his words and actions. Then you would be more likely to believe his words.

Any time either partner questions the level of commitment, the partners can shift to conversing to work out details. Partners may also choose to metacommunicate, a specific form of conversing, to uncover details about how commitment is talked about or to shed light on the nonverbals that indicate commitment (or lack of it). Overall, the goal with interpersonal commitment is to be as comfortable as possible with one another, knowing you can really count on and trust that person.

A different but related type of commitment is the partners' commitment to the partnership. That is, partners need to be committed to working together in ways that work for them both. Like other kinds of commitment, partnership commitment can change over time as circumstances change at the personal, professional, or institutional level. Whenever this happens, partners may revisit the verbal, written, or implied commitments to make modifications or to reaffirm the original agreements. In short, when in doubt (about commitment), check it out!

Another necessary level of commitment for community-based partnerships involves the commitment to members of the community and their needs. When each partner really cares about the people in the community and their lives, the possibilities for working together are enhanced. But when one partner is only trying to get a particular job done, others may question his or her motives and long-term commitment. Unfortunately, this can set up tensions between campus and community members and needs to be addressed before doing sustainable partnership work. (The story about the Edgecombe County–ECU partnership at the end of chapter 1 is a great example of the kind of commitment necessary to make lasting change.)

Organizational-level commitments between campuses and communities help clarify roles, responsibilities, and the ways partners work together, as well as meet legal requirements. Partners at other levels should have some awareness of official interorganizational ground rules so there is consistency between what is intended and what actually happens.

The various layers of commitment can impact two partners' daily work in profound ways. For instance, tensions or conflicts at the organizational level may need to be addressed for the partners to work optimally together. For example, when the partners want to share using a new technology that is not approved or supported at the university, partners could run into technical issues without a clear place to turn for help. Interestingly enough, the impacts of different levels of commitment have been addressed in the frameworks for engaged campuses promoted by Holland (2005) and others. (See chapter 7 for more information about managing differences or conflicts.)

Take-Away Lessons About Committing

- Commitment involves choices that lay a foundation of expectations between partners.
- Commitments happen at multiple levels (between organizations, between organizations and communities, between partners, and between partners and the community). All of these influence the partners and their work.
- Specific agreements may need to be revisited or revised when circumstances or partners change in order for the collaboration to stay dynamic and innovative.
- A solid commitment by partners can make a partnership; the lack of commitment by partners can break a partnership.

Looking Deeper at the Elements: Partner Patterns

Partner patterns refers to the collection of communication practices and guidelines developed uniquely between two or more partners. These patterns help partners develop a shared past and present and provide a base to work together in sustained ways in the future.

Partner patterns can develop both verbally and nonverbally. Experiences together can allow partners to use a word, short phrase, or signal to swiftly recall a special memory and related unique meanings. Think about a close relationship and ways that you quickly check in with the other person (i.e., connect). You may refer to a private joke. You may use a nonverbal symbol (e.g., that shirt with the colorful logo that you created together on vacation). Such partner patterns help you get a quick read on one another when you next get together.

Similarly, community-campus partners' quick ways to connect become part of their shared relational history over time. Some form partnership rituals that become a part of their common "partnership identity" (see Janke, 2009).

For instance, when Rocco and Gracie met to go to the Habitat for Humanity construction site together, they used an established partnership pattern. Each one said, "What's up?" and they simultaneously reached skyward to slap hands quickly. This communication ritual allowed them to check in with each other and create a positive vibe as they headed out together for their service-learning class project.

Another partner pattern might come through a story, where partners readily understand some shared value or belief. For example, when Angel and Augusto were talking at the soup kitchen, they started sharing their family experiences with cooking and found out that both had grandmothers who home-canned local produce. Later, when things got really hectic in the kitchen, Angel said, "Well, at least we aren't dealing with exploding jars of tomatoes like my grandma did." Augusto responded, "We can deal with the pressure in this kitchen! It's nothing like using that pressure cooker pot my granny did." Both laughed. Their stories about their grandmas became a way to release tension and increase laughter as they worked together.

Similarly, Sarah and Dr. Aaron were talking one day and discovered they both owned black Labrador Retrievers. This led to regularly sharing dog photos and laughing at the antics of their pets.

Dr. Aaron said, "No matter what happens at work, when I go home Lucy looks at me with those soft eyes and wags her tail furiously. My troubles just melt." Sarah responded, "I know what you mean. Brooks can lift my spirits in an instant when he runs to the door to greet me."

These shared experiences with Labs helped form a relational theme: No matter what happens, we always get some love from our dogs. Such stories and the related theme helped them realize they could power through difficulties together and then go home to get some love from Lucy and Brooks.

Other examples of relational themes might include statements like the following: "We are partners no matter what happens!" "I'll be there for you even after we finish our work together." (*Note*: These are relational themes and demonstrate commitment between partners.) Those statements between partners help solidify the partnership and provide positive promise for the future of a long-term, lasting relationship.

Take-Away Lessons About Partner Patterns

- Partner patterns develop verbally or nonverbally through shared relational experiences.
- Partner patterns create unique meanings between two people that make their partnership distinct.
- When using partner patterns, we tap into a shared past or present to provide a base for interactions in the future.

For more information, including examples, see Table 3.1.

Limitations and Cautions for Collaborative Communication

The collaborative communication framework assumes the basic values of mutuality, reciprocity, shared power, ethical awareness, and cultural sensitivities common to community engagement. So the underlying definition of *collaboration* used throughout this book purposely excludes negative, unethical communication that knowingly ignores the interests of community members or other partners.

Realistically, though, there are times when full-fledged collaborative communication must be limited or just isn't possible. For instance, when one partner's safety is in jeopardy, boundaries may be needed to establish what partners can talk about and what is off limits. Safety comes first!

At other times, partners may not be able to commit to full collaboration but still want to be involved in some aspect of the community-campus work. This may happen in a new partnership that hasn't yet fully determined the long-term course of what they will do together. In that case, some elements of the collaborative communication framework may prove helpful. (See also ideas in the appendix.)

TABLE 3.1
Collaborative Communication Specifies

Type	Definition	Key Purpose	How It Works	Challenges	Benefits	Examples
Connect	Communication to find common ground to establish rapport and closeness with partner	To create a deeper bond or closeness between partners	Uses verbal or nonverbal communication or a combination	Can take time and detective work to find best ways to connect with each partner based on his or her needs, ways of learning, and so on	Creates partnership bond; can help partners in times of stress or difficulties	Reference to funny shared experience causes partners to laugh; note or e-mail to say that the partner is cared for
Converse	Interactive dialogue or exchange that goes back and forth between partners	To foster understanding by sharing information or exploring ideas, or even talking through differences	Requires verbal communication, which can be modified, supplemented, or contradicted by nonverbals	Can be misunderstood; takes time to check perceptions or ask questions to clarify; metacommunication sometimes needed	Primary way to learn; allows partners to contribute ideas or expertise related to issue or projects	"I wanted you to know that I found a number of resources online that relate to our work. Let's review them together." "Could you explain why you were upset with me the last time we met?"

Envision	Dreams for community, crystallizing possibilities into words and pictures that gradually focus efforts into targeted, doable actions	To come up with a vision for what's possible together and then to define specific goals and actions of partnership aligned with a larger vision	Involves both verbal and nonverbal communication to establish action steps; end product can be written, visual, or both	Requires both fluid and crystalline intelligences, expertise and talents of multiple people, risk-taking and creative courage to work collaboratively on a vision that works for all	Knowledge that community changes are desired and many steps are needed to get there; useful for input and awareness by community members to get buy-in; basis for stories when aligned with completed steps and accomplishments	End products, mission statements, program priorities, program of work summary, vision boards or visuals of end goals and what "success" will look like
Commit	Agreements by partners, organizations, and communities about roles, responsibilities, and ways partners will work together	To determine the structure and functions of the partnership	Can be verbal or written, often including five Ws and one H (who, what, when, where, why, and how)	Can have differences among individual, organizational, or community-centered commitments; may change with time or different circumstances	Helps build basis for understanding rules, roles, and basic responsibilities	MOUs; verbal decision by partners to work together to achieve a specific set of goals
Partner Patterns	Collection of communication practices and processes unique to partners	To create the past, present, and future of the partnership relationship as a base for future work together	Verbal and nonverbal	Often based on shared experiences and recognition of uniqueness rather than on planned patterns	Creates unique sense of who partners are together and forms a "partnership identity"	Unique words, phrases, or symbols that partners use that have specific meanings; could also be shared rituals, themes of the relationship and so on

Happily, though, in many community-campus engagement efforts, higher levels of collaboration are possible and highly recommended. All elements of the collaborative communication framework can then feed into the partners' relationship.

A Collaborative Communication Repertoire: Pragmatics

Different types of communication have been teased apart in the collaborative communication framework to distinguish between kinds of communication that partners enact to have a dynamic, sustainable partnership. This proves useful as partners work to build a viable collaborative communication repertoire.

In practice, though, the framework elements are interrelated and flow in a continuous thread or spiral of communication between partners as detailed in chapter 2. Moreover, when partners communicate, some communication practices or processes will impact different parts of the framework, so the elements are not fully distinct or mutually exclusive. That is, one set of verbal statements could fall into two different elements or categories of the collaborative communication framework. Still, the elements detailed throughout this book provide the basis for ongoing learning and capacity-building about how to collaborate well.

Importantly, many other writings about collaboration from multiple disciplines highlight the importance of well-developed repertoires of competent communication. Indeed, some argue that collaboration is in essence communication (see Hardy et al., 2005; Heath & Frey, 2004; Lewis, 2006). That is, collaboration requires a mutuality mind-set and related communication that reflects the key ethics and values of community engagement. So collaborative communication isn't just nice to use in our community-campus partnerships; it's absolutely necessary!

The Collaborative Communication Framework: Extended Example

Because collaborative communication is built on creative capacities and multiple elements, a nearly infinite number of possibilities for collaborative communication exist. The following story is just one example of how the collaborative communication framework elements could work together.

Nani wanted to work with others to develop a program to pick up refuse along roads in her city. To really make a difference, though, she recognized that multiple people would need to take on the program long term rather than setting up a onetime cleanup event. She also recognized that her ideas were good but that when others got involved, things might change. She might even change herself!

So she went to her friend Sasha, the local director of an after-school program, and shared the idea with her. Nani and Sasha already had a *connection* because they were friends, but their common interests in caring for their community added to the *connecting* bond. They talked about how much they both cared about the environment and also thought it was important to teach kids about environmental matters at an early age.

In addition, Sasha could readily see the benefits for the after-school kids of getting out and helping others. She told Nani it would provide even stronger learning for her kids if the university was involved somehow.

Nani and Sasha *conversed* about those things and also shared information about people they knew on campus who might be interested. Nani's first choice was Dennis, the director of the civic engagement program on campus. He knew all kinds of people across campus and would likely help them network and start *connecting* with others. So Nani agreed to talk to Dennis. Sasha thought it would be great to have someone from campus come talk to her kids about environmentalism and added that idea to the *conversation*. Nani then remembered another organization, Got Science, that was geared toward getting kids involved in science and mentioned it to Sasha. She'd ask Dennis about that, too.

During the initial *conversation* between Nani and Dennis, he suggested setting up a meeting to *envision* the possibilities of joint work. Once the meeting time and place were set up, he would *converse* with some of the groups on campus to get key people to attend. He would also ask Got Science if they could provide easy-to-understand lessons for kids of different ages about environmental topics, including why picking up trash mattered. Nani thought his ideas were great and had another *conversation* with Sasha to fill her in. They realized that the initial ideas they had might be reshaped as they went along, but they were okay with that.

Sasha's budget allowed her to provide good snacks and other food that really helped bring folks out to the *envisioning* time. Fun activities were planned that allowed Sasha, Nani, and Dennis to compile ideas. They captured some of the visuals that were drawn using cell phone photos, including snapshots of the flipchart where the group had recorded key ideas.

This meeting time got things off to a good start and two of the student groups wanted to stay involved over the long haul, so they talked about the level of *commitment* that was possible for them over several years. Sasha also agreed that she would *commit* to having several groups of kids from the after-school program involved on alternate trash pickup days for a number of years.

The collaborative communication continued from there. In time, partners developed *partner patterns* such as shared stories about how much fun it was to work together and the theme that they could make a difference by working together developed. Nani's good idea sparked collaborative communication that began an environmentally oriented program that improved the city, taught the children more about environmental concerns, and gradually expanded beyond that city to neighboring ones.

Take-Away Lessons About Collaborative Communication

- Collaboration involves challenging, dynamic communication with the potential for partners to transform communities for the common good.
- Collaborative communication requires capacity-building and mindful learning for partners across the life of the partnership.
- Creating change with others is likely to require changes within us.

Putting Chapter Ideas Into Action

Action for Partnerships and Teaching About Partnerships

1. In practice, connecting can happen multiple ways. Meeting in person or interacting via webcam or other visuals may be essential for some partners to connect well. This may lead toward phone calls or verbal chats online using audio conferencing or other technological innovations. As an activity, have students (or others) think about the methods of connection that suit them best and compile that information to generate a list of connecting practices. Questions to stimulate discussion include the following: What is it that happens communicatively when you feel closest to someone who matters in your life? What verbals work best? What nonverbals make you feel cared about? How do you think these might work for different kinds of partners based on your past community-based experiences?

2. Individuals may specialize primarily in fluid or crystalline intelligence. We recognize this when we call one person an "idea generator" (i.e., skilled with fluid intelligence) and another "the voice of reason" (i.e., skilled with crystalline intelligence). Conversations between students or

partners could identify which kind of intelligence comes most readily to the individuals involved. Then they could converse about how they might share their go-to ways of thinking in a group situation or with another partner.

Action for Community-Engaged Scholarship

1. Each element in the collaborative communication framework is worthy of research specific to community-campus partnerships. For instance, important questions to ask might include the following: What are the best ways for partners to connect? What kinds of envisioning communication yields results that seem to capture ideas quickly so they can be reviewed or retrieved later? Research results for these pragmatic kinds of questions hold real possibilities for capacity-building and identifying effective daily practices among campus and community partners as they go about their work.

2. The engagement literature often refers to "open communication"— a murky concept that lacks precision and clear meaning. Gaining a better understanding of the nature of open communication as it relates to community engagement might be very useful. For instance, when participants say they want open communication, do they actually mean partners' willingness to communicate? Or do participants mean a scheduled meeting that is inclusive of various community and campus members? Or are they considering a free-flowing kind of conversation where there are no barriers to communicating? Answers to questions like these could provide meaningful and useful insights for all of us.

4

PRACTICES AND PROCESSES FOR COLLABORATIVE COMMUNICATION

Communication is a skill that you can learn. It's like riding a bicycle or typing. If you're willing to work at it, you can rapidly improve the quality of every part of your life.

—Brian Tracy

The bicycle metaphor for communication can be carried a little further. Like riding a bicycle, communicating with others can be fun, once you master some of the basics. Further, like riding a bike with others, using your collaborative communication repertoire with others can lead you on fascinating journeys!

This chapter focuses on some best practices and processes for partnerships and collaborative communication. These are good starting places to build a ready-to-use repertoire. Then you can add other communication knowledge and skills later as you continue on your journey. Always keep in mind the need to be flexible and adapt to the person and to the situation, so you can continue the journey even when obstacles or unexpected situations arise.

Connecting by Listening Carefully

Listening well is powerful communication when you offer your full presence to another. Think about how much it means to you when a parent or a friend stops everything else to really listen to what is happening in your life, especially when you are stressed. Something similar can happen when you really listen to others.

Unfortunately, though, listening well is too often neglected or over-looked. We've all been there. A young man once pointed out to me that I wasn't really listening. I parroted back every single word the man had just uttered. Still, he pointed out that no eye contact had been made between us so "real" listening was *not* happening. True enough. Listening with the whole self matters, especially when the other really wants or needs to be heard.

People don't always think of listening as communication, but it is. As mentioned in the section on mindful listening in chapter 3, good listening, or *ting*, involves more than just hearing words (Ting-Toomey & Chung, 2012, p. 199). Hearing is the physical process of taking sound vibrations into one's brain and converting them into meaning. Active listening, in contrast, draws on both auditory and visual cues. Listening well involves hearing/receiving, attending, understanding, responding, and recalling information (Adler, Rosenfeld, & Proctor, 2007).

For example, Mae thought Mark was one of the best listeners she had ever met, so she asked if he had any listening secrets to share. Mark said he focused his whole self on hearing and watching another person (i.e., receiving). He tended to be aware of the nuances of the words as well as the energy behind them as he received information.

He pointed out that he was a relational listener because he focused on establishing commonalities with the other person to understand his or her emotions (Bodie, Worthington, & Gearhart, 2013) as well as his or her words. Mae could believe that! When she talked with him, she felt heard—like he got her far beyond the words she said. This attentiveness (i.e., attending) felt great to her so she became excited when talking with Mark. He picked up on this and mirrored back the high energy and enthusiasm she used (i.e., responding). Sometimes he asked questions to make sure he understood her (i.e., understanding).

The other thing that amazed Mae about Mark's listening was that he always seemed to remember what she told him long after they talked (i.e., recalling). His secret? Mark used mnemonics, or memory devices, to store information accurately.

He shared a quick story to explain: "During my freshman year, I had to learn about ancient peoples in my anthropology class. Names like Neanderthals, Cro-Magnons, and others weren't easy to remember. So I created a catchy little tune and aligned the names with the different sounds of the music. Bet I can still remember it." Mark began to sing the names. Mae thought this was pretty funny, so funny she could hardly stop laughing to continue their conversation.

The best listening involves a firm intent to gather information using those four listening steps. Not all listening is equal, though. Four kinds of listeners have been identified: relational listeners (like Mark), task-oriented listeners, analytical listeners, and critical listeners (see Bodie et al., 2013). Task-oriented listeners want specific information to make decisions or to inform actions, so they want to stick with the topic and avoid "irrelevant" details. In contrast, analytical listeners want lots of information so they can understand the topic from many different perspectives—to get the full picture. Critical listeners, though, want to check the accuracy and consistency in messages and do a specialized kind of "fact checking" whenever they listen.

Each type of listening has strengths and weaknesses. Relational listeners can bond with others deeply, but task-oriented listeners glean what they need to get things done. Analytical listeners consider all sides of a topic, but critical listeners focus on accurate, consistent, and verifiable information. With practice, you can learn to use all of these various kinds of listening to meet a particular purpose when you communicate with partners. This also helps build your communication repertoire. Learn more by reviewing the listening styles in Table 4.1.

Connecting via Different Media: Assets and Deficits

Sometimes active listening is not an option when partners use social media like texts or Twitter or e-mail. That means auditory information (including tone of voice or inflections or energy behind the words) won't be available to make meaning. Texts, Twitter, and e-mail are also devoid of facial expressions, posture, and gestures. Instead they focus on words (i.e., text based) despite sometimes including pictures.

But, as noted in chapter 2, nonverbals tend to carry social and emotional information. So communicators can supplement text-based messages to build social and emotional understanding between partners. Metacommunication (communication about communication) can help flesh out what works best for the partners and the partnership at a given time and for a particular purpose.

Text-based message media do have big advantages because of immediacy (i.e., instantaneous transmission), personal convenience, and sharing across great distances, forgoing traditional group boundaries. For busy partners, these advantages make texting, for instance, quite valuable for communicating.

Other social media like Instagram or Pinterest rely heavily on visual information. Although not used to chat, these visually based social media channels can be valuable for sharing pictures or drawings or other visual information that the partners wish to exchange. These features could be

TABLE 4.1
Listening Styles Chart

Style Name	Key Characteristics	Strengths	Limitations	Suggestions
Relational	Individual tends to focus on understanding the emotions of others; wants to connect with others and have them "feel understood."	Very oriented toward relationship building and using emotional intelligence. Useful in promoting the partnership, especially during stress.	Could be overfocused on the relationship and miss other kinds of incoming information.	Watch for contexts and situations that might need more "content" information. Learn to use other styles when beneficial to partners or the work.
Analytical	Individual tends to withhold judgment and consider all sides of an issue or all aspects of a person's perspective; wants the "whole message."	Very in-depth approach. Useful to identify multiple perspectives/contexts that could affect the partnership.	Could be too focused on the big picture of a conversation and miss important "minor" details.	Watch for a particular set of details or message elements that are critical to the partner or the partnership in the current situation.
Task Oriented	Individual tends to see a listening transaction as a "task" to be completed; wants to stay focused and "on topic."	Very goal oriented. Useful to move partnership goals forward.	Could be overfocused on getting listening done and miss partnership information.	Watch for ways to stay involved with listening to others and more fully connected to them, not just to the content being shared.
Critical Listening	Individual tends to watch for accuracy and consistency when listening to others.	Very logic oriented. Could help identify areas of concern that partners may need to address.	Could be so focused on accuracy that the other partner may not want to talk.	Watch for ways to listen without judgments to what matters to the partner in terms of both content and the relationship.

Notes. Listening styles are habitual ways or individual preferences to receive and process incoming information. Use this table to define where you are as a partner now and to identify what might help the partnership work better.

Author's note. Table developed by author based on listening styles and characteristics found in Bodie et al., 2013. The strengths, limitations, and suggestions are the author's (see also Watson, Barker, & Weaver, 1995).

useful, for instance, when planning a community event or a project where partners need to share visual ideas "in the works."

A multitude of media tools that partners could use to connect offers both auditory and visual cues—such as short videos created by a webcam or smartphone, or talking by using Skype or Facetime. These multichannel forms are richer in terms of the kinds of data they offer partners. Some are synchronous (i.e., in real time) and can allow partners to get together and share virtually when they can't meet in person. Others are asynchronous (i.e., available for use at a time when the partner is available). A webinar, for instance, could be used for one partner to share training needed for their joint work so the partner could watch/listen when it was convenient and fit into his or her schedule.

Media message forms vary in their richness or how many cues communicators can use to understand messages. What's most important in terms of your communication repertoire is to recognize partner needs and preferences and find ways to share messages that fit the partner's circumstances and capabilities. (Remember from chapter 1 when Rachel wanted to connect with Shannon via Skype but that didn't work for him. They both had good reasons for their preferences, so a partner conversation and subsequent decision was needed.)

It's important to realize that all communicators must choose how to share messages both interpersonally and using media sources. (Table 2.1 can help with making this choice.)

Conversing: Fostering Supportive Communication

Another important aspect of building great partnerships is to use supportive communication. Specifically, supportive communication involves verbal or nonverbal communication that intentionally provides assistance (Burleson & MacGeorge, 2002) and caring to create "environments in which individuals feel secure and encouraged to seek good solutions" (Shockley-Zalabak, 2015, p. 308). Five different types of supportive communication have been identified between spouses (Cutrona & Suhr, 1992) that are relevant to community-engaged partners: emotional support, esteem support, informational support, tangible aid, and network support.

Emotional support uses expressions of caring, concern, and empathy. For example, when noticing that the partner is acting differently, one might say, "I notice that you seem down today. Just want you to know that I really care about you. Would you like a hug?"

Esteem support makes another person feel valued, admired, and capable. As an example consider a statement such as the following: "Wow! You did a great job explaining your agency to the students. You really know your stuff!"

Informational support gives advice or information that might help someone solve a problem. For instance, "Would you like to know what I think might help?" (Waits for answer to be affirmative. If so, continues.) "You might consider sending your message through an e-mail newsletter so people get it sooner than one mailed out."

Tangible aid provides assistance, goods, or services needed. For example, after local flooding, business leaders asked what would be most useful. Then people in their organizations gathered those items to help the people in the community who were impacted.

Network support directs the person to someone who can help based on similar experiences or specific needs. In the flooding example, a campus partner might say, "I know someone in the Geography Department who might be able to help you get the maps you need drawn for your project. Would you like me to connect you via e-mail so you can discuss possibilities?"

In short, supportive communication can provide a positive space for free-flowing interactions between partners, because it feels safe to "put myself out there" through communication with the other. Supportive communication is vital to connecting; it can also be used with other elements in the collaborative communication framework.

Defensive communication, in contrast, tends to focus on limiting the participation of others or controlling the situation in some way. Often, defensive communication is used to protect the self (or the team)—similar to being "on the defensive" in football or other sports. Four types of defensive communication have been identified: dogmatic messages, superiority messages, indifference messages, and control messages (Waldron, Turner, Alexander, & Barton, 1993).

Dogmatic messages dismiss ideas or suggestions by passing judgment on the other's thinking or actions, making the speaker's own ideas the only viable choices. For example, one partner might claim, "Why should I change my behavior to suit you? This way has always worked for me in the past." Superiority messages claim special abilities, power, or status that supersedes anything the other person might have. For instance, a supervisor might say, "Since I'm the boss, you have to do what I say. Frankly, it doesn't matter what you think." Indifference messages show disregard and rejection of the other's ideas as being unimportant or even irrelevant. For example, imagine two students talking about their group project for class. One of them might say, "My idea is best. Why would you think yours would work?" Control messages take charge of either the situation or the other person. At a meeting, one controlling person might point out, "The only reasonable way to proceed is to shorten the time that we spend together. Anything else is not acceptable."

Defensive messages like these can decrease trust between partners, making it hard to work together effectively, especially if they are used consistently. Visually, you can picture supportive communication and defensive communication as sitting on opposite ends of a line in terms of whether they encourage mutual sharing. Supportive communication promotes two-way sharing; defensive communication limits back-and-forth sharing and tends to be one-way. In collaborative partnerships, much of the communication will fall toward the supportive end of that line, because supportive communication tends to promote positive relational climates.

Still, choices must be made. One-way communication might be appropriate when we are reacting to a perceived threat or a need to put up protective boundaries. Taking control over the situation is essential then. For example, if campus buildings were on lockdown because of a shooter being sighted, people on campus would be on guard. Outgoing and incoming information would be limited. As another example, consider that a community organization working with battered women and children might rightfully limit information (i.e., sharing) about their clients, such as their whereabouts.

When supportive communication is used most of the time, we can move forward with confidence that, even though we don't know what may happen in the future, the partnership itself is something we can count on. To be innovative in our community engagement work, this reliability is what we want and need.

One caution, though: Like all forms of communication, using what we think is supportive verbally or nonverbally doesn't always mean the other person will interpret the message as supportive. All of us interpret information based upon our field of experience as well as our initial understandings of the words and nonverbals used. That's why a full repertoire of communication possibilities helps us make choices so that, over time, we can build in-depth understanding with partners.

Shockley-Zalabak (2015) has detailed six practices that help build supportive communication in a business or organizational setting. These could be readily applied in a community engagement context instead.

First, *describe* the problem or situation (rather than evaluate or judge the problem/situation and the person connected with it). Descriptions involve sharing facts without judgments about what those facts mean. When describing, any internal interpretations are held loosely, so they can be changed as additional information alters our initial conceptions.

For example, Jose, a community partner, couldn't figure out why he hadn't heard back from the student (Kim) working with him on a fund-raising campaign after sending her multiple e-mails. Rather than judging that Kim didn't care about their work, Jose phoned and left a message. In that message, he described the facts, that he had sent several e-mails with no response, and said he needed immediate feedback in order to continue the fund-raising project.

Kim called him back right away. She said her e-mail had been hacked and her computer was in the campus computer center for repairs, so she hadn't gotten those messages. (Now the lack of response to his e-mails became clearer to Jose.) They went on to talk about next steps for their joint project and figured out alternate ways to communicate. That worked! The fund-raiser was held two short weeks later.

Second, *work together* to solve a problem or an issue rather than have the solution imposed or forced on partners or team members by someone with greater power. This stance helps us assume "we will work together to solve this issue rather than turning to someone else." To illustrate, Melinda was really tempted to go to her professor because her group wasn't creating the logo she thought was best for the partner agency in their class project. Surely the professor had the grade power to get her groupmates to think twice! But, she'd just learned about supportive communication in another class and decided to try that approach with her group members instead.

At the group's next scheduled meeting, Melinda suggested that group members share several draft logo drawings with their partner, Marco, to let him decide which one was best. She pointed out that the group could produce a great final product that met the organization's needs because it got advance approval. (This approach also allowed her to share the newer logo that she thought might work.)

They met with Marco the next day. He suggested using the one most group members liked, but he also wanted to integrate one portion of Melinda's favorite in the final version. Group members were amazed because they hadn't shared anything about their prior group conversations with Marco. But, after the meeting, they creatively incorporated all the elements Marco wanted into an attractive design that visually conveyed the intended message quickly. In the end, everyone was happy.

Third, *be transparent* about motives and reasons for thoughts, actions, or policies rather than try to manipulate another person. This means sharing "why" things are done rather than implementing strategies or practices unilaterally so they come across as orders or mandates from one person.

In the situation with Melinda and her group, Marco was transparent about what worked and why. He explained to group members that combining parts of two drawings would allow the finished logo to be culturally appropriate to the people served while still conveying the purposes of his organization to others.

Fourth, *empathize* about what is happening for the other person rather than try to stay neutral and objective all the time. In other words, be caring and willing to learn so that the partner is more likely to express opinions and beliefs as well as information. Showing caring can also be very important in terms of establishing a sense of equality, trust, and mutual benefit between partners.

Consider the following situation: Linner was worried because the building where her clients in wheelchairs met was flooded, making it inaccessible. When she told her board of directors about the problem, the board president said, "Linner, tell us more. You always do a great job for our clients, but this is a tough one. Maybe if we work together with campus experts and local businesses we can find a short-term fix and a long-term solution, too." After that, Linner was relieved. She was sure glad the board members cared about more than just the facts.

Fifth, *approach others as equals* rather than assert superiority for some kind of expertise or experience. Soon, Linner reached out to Emily, the director of civic engagement on a nearby campus, to see if she could identify faculty and students with expertise to redesign the building one board member had found. As the faculty members and students began to work with Linner, they saw she understood her clients and their needs far better than they could. So they all worked together as equals to develop workable plans for the building.

Sixth, *be willing to learn and explore possibilities* for behavior, attitudes, and ideas rather than take a dogmatic approach to what must happen. For instance, in the planning process for the building, the architecture and design students suggested having a group meeting with volunteer clients eager to use the new space to learn more rather than just relying on their own ideas. Linner thought this was great. During the meeting, students gleaned ideas from the people who would actually use the building as well as applied what they'd learned in class. This approach worked well for all—the students brought out their best expertise (the "me") yet worked together well with the others (the "we"). Linner and the clients knew that the students cared about their individual ideas (the "me") and how the design would work best for them as a group (the "we').

Find a useful quick reference to these ideas in Table 4.2.

TABLE 4.2
Supportive and Defensive Communication Summary

Supportive Communication Practices	*Build positive communication climates, trust, well-being of partners/partnership*
Description	Share observations without added judgments/evaluations
Problem Orientation	Focus on what partners can do together to address issue or problem
Spontaneity	Be flexible and adaptable depending on the situation and other person's needs and wants
Empathy	Recognize verbally or nonverbally the other person's needs, views, wants (demonstrates caring)
Equality	Promote both partners' involvement and contributions without preference for just one
Provisionalism	Hold own ideas and opinions loosely and be willing to change if more information makes another view more reasonable
Defensive Communication Practices	*If used consistently promote negative communication climate; limit sharing through one-way flow of information*
Evaluation	Judge other person and information shared negatively, often using "you" language and lacking specifics
Control	Impose solution or ideas with little regard for the other's ideas, thoughts, or feelings
Strategy	Plan to achieve set outcome and "sell" one's own position; often seen as win-lose approach
Neutrality/ Indifference	Show a lack of interest or concern for other; imply that the other isn't as important
Superiority	Convey own expertise or experience or status without recognizing the potential contributions of another
Certainty	Make invariable statements that show lack of regard for other's information or views
Supportive Message Practices	
Emotional Support	Verbal/nonverbal expressions of caring, concern, empathy
Esteem Support	Expressions recognizing another person's value or capabilities

(Continues)

TABLE 4.2. (*Continued*)

Informational Support	Verbal advice or information to solve a problem
Tangible Aid	Offers of goods, services, or other assistance supplied to the other
Network Support	Verbal sharing about people who could help provide expertise or similar experiences
Defensive Message Types	
Dogmatic Messages	Dismiss the other's ideas or information, making the speaker's own view the only "real possibility"
Superiority Messages	Claim own power, status, or expertise as more valuable, superseding the other's
Indifference Messages	Show disregard for other and rejection of ideas and information he or she shares
Control Messages	Take charge of the other and the situation without discussion or any flexibility allowed

Note: There is some overlap between the practices and the message types. Still, they align well in terms of our understandings of relational/partnership outcomes.
Source: Communication practices based on Gibbs (1961); see also Adler et al. (2007) for related research. Supportive message types based on Cutrona and Suhr (1992). Defensive message types based on Waldron et al. (1993).

Conversing: Multiple Messages in Each Conversation

As you can see, communication can be complicated. But there's more. Each and every time people communicate interpersonally, there are multiple messages shared. There is a content message, a relational message, and an identity message embedded in each face-to-face communication.

Content-level messages consist of information about the topic(s). Content messages are typically shared verbally. When a person says, "Please be more direct" and "Say what you mean" or "Stick to the facts please," the focus is on the content-level message.

Along with the content message, though, comes information about how the communicating partner feels about the other, summing up the current "state of the relationship" (Ting-Toomey & Chung, 2012, p. 27). Relational messages may not be obvious. Ting-Toomey and Chung (2012) point out that "relational meaning is inferred via nonverbal intonations, body movements, or gestures that accompany the verbal content" (p. 27) of the message. So, for instance, a nonverbally based relational message of leaning toward the other person might indicate how much the partner is appreciated and valued.

Another level of meaning, the identity meaning, gets at how we conceptualize ourselves and our partnership. "Identity meaning involves issues such as the display of respect or disrespect and identity approval or disapproval" (Ting-Toomey & Chung, 2012, p. 27). In a dyadic partnership, respect matters for both people to stay "all in" as they work collaboratively. For example, when one partner says she is stressed, the other can reach out to touch her hand while saying softly, "We're in this together."

When receiving information, people typically "infer identity meanings through the speaker's tone of voice, facial expressions, nonverbal postures, spatial distance, and selective word choices. Nonverbal tones or gestures, however, are highly culture dependent and (can be) easily misinterpreted" (Ting-Toomey & Chung, 2012, p. 27). Consequently, it's important for partners to double-check the meanings of nonverbals to ensure greater shared understanding, especially when it comes to relational and identity messages.

Collaborating Practices: Check Meaning to Build Understanding

As humans, we cannot mind read to fully "understand what another person thinks, feels, or perceives" (Wood, 2007, p. 91). Because of limited cues and our variations in interpreting, incomplete understanding is *always* what we should expect when communicating. Still, to avoid imposing our own ideas, feelings, and perceptions on others, we must aim to get the best mutual understanding possible. Perception checks and paraphrases can help us see if the meaning received is close to what the sender intended. Metacommunication, or communication about communication, can help determine what communication is working well between partners and what may need to change.

Perception checks involve stating what you have noticed or heard and then asking whether the other perceives the same thing (Wood, 2007). For instance, you might tell a partner, "When I saw you cross your arms and sigh, I thought you didn't want to listen to me anymore. Is that right?" The partner might respond, "No. I really want to hear what you have to share. But it's really cold in here so I crossed my arms. The sigh was because the thermostat is in another office! Let's go somewhere else to continue our talk." Perception checks involve both mindful listening and openness and can generate a conversation to clarify the meaning and intent of the verbal and nonverbal information received.

Perception checks can also help resolve mixed messages, when the words and nonverbals seem to convey different things. Research shows that nonverbals typically speak louder than words. That is, if people perceive a discrepancy between words and actions or between words and other nonverbals, they will tend to believe the nonverbals.

The following example shows the use of a perception check to address a perceived mixed message. Lealand noticed that his organizational partner, Patrice, kept looking at the clock on her smartphone and scribbling on a paper as their group meeting continued. Even so, she kept up her end of the conversation, regularly contributing ideas and suggestions. She seemed fully engaged, but the watch behavior was confusing. Finally, Lealand said, "Hey, Patrice, what's up with looking at the clock? Do you have an appointment somewhere else that you need to get to?" Patrice laughed as she responded, "Not at all. My boss asked me to do a time study so we can better use the time I'm at work, especially when I'm out of the office." Mixed meaning solved!

Paraphrasing, another communication skill, involves the receiver restating the message in new words. This process can allow the original speaker to restate the content of his or her message or clarify intent, potentially adding new information to affirm or to alter the recipient's understanding. For example, a community partner might note, "I heard you say that you were ready to write down ideas to pitch for a feature story about our partnership. Did I understand you right?" The journalism student could respond affirmatively or offer a clarification or correction of the paraphrase—for example, "Yeah, I want to do a feature story, but I'm not sure I can take it on alone. Let's take a minute to brainstorm some ideas together." Afterward, the student might ask, "Are you willing to be involved in an interview after I make the pitch to another student so we can work together?"

Paraphrasing works well when stated in "tentative language" (Wood, 2007). When we state our paraphrase tentatively, it signals to our partner that we recognize the potential to be incorrect in understanding what he or she has said and is willing to change. For instance, one might begin, "I thought I heard you say . . ." (using tentative language) rather than stating definitively, "You said . . ." A tentative approach lets the partner know that we want to be sure about what exactly is being said. This approach also focuses attention on the partner's ideas rather than back on the listener or on the listener's interpretation. Paraphrasing can be a great way to nurture the partner and the partnership because paraphrasing demonstrates the key community engagement values of reciprocity and respect.

Metacommunication is another good way to check out meaning. Despite popular press articles and books about "body language" having very specific meanings, communication scholars recognize that nonverbal communication can be ambiguous, culturally bound, and all too easily misunderstood (Ting-Toomey & Chung, 2012; Wood, 2007). So asking what a particular facial expression or gesture means can go a long way toward promoting mutual understanding and building a positive relational climate.

We can also use metacommunication to check out whether a particular way of sending a message is best for the partner—for example, "I sent you an e-mail last week to update you on the project. Does that form of communication work well or would you prefer something else?" Metacommunication can be useful in routine, everyday interactions but is particularly important when working with people who have different communication styles or preferences. Metacommunication is also vital during boundary spanning, as shown by the following examples: "In your organization, what kind of communication do you use most often to send messages to other employees?"; "When you are trying to get information out to the people you serve in the community, what have you found works the best?" Find out more by reviewing Table 4.3.

Confirming meanings with your partners using perception checks, paraphrasing, and metacommunication can help build goodwill between partners. In addition, these are useful communication practices to glean additional data that builds greater understanding across the lifetime of the partnership. So when in doubt about what you saw or heard, ask! But even when you have no doubt, it may be helpful to double-check your understanding rather than mindlessly make assumptions or interpretations that might not be quite accurate.

Social Change, Communication, and the Need for Trust

No matter what communication they use, community-engaged partners work to produce community-focused change. Change can be seen as a major challenge or, alternately, as an opportunity in the making. How we look at it may be shaped by how much a change impacts us or those closest to us. Rosabeth Moss Kanter says, "Change is disturbing when it is done to us, exhilarating when it is done by us" (quoted in Holman, Devane, & Cady, 2008, p. i).

Many interpersonal dynamics come into play during times of change, such as when the partnership and the partners themselves are in flux. Shifra Sered discovered, "Partnership . . . is about vulnerably opening yourself up to the possibility that the relationship formed will change you" (personal communication, spring 2014). During 2013–2014, Sered, as part of the AmeriCorps VISTA program, served at ECU to facilitate a partnership between ECU

TABLE 4.3

Metacommunication (Communication on Communication) in Collaborative Communication

Collaborative Communication Framework Element	Some Metacommunication Uses	Examples
Connecting	• Find "best" ways to connect with target readers/audience in a particular situation. • Identify preferred ways a partner likes to connect. • Discover when might be good times to connect.	How could we best share information about our new project with people in the community? What are some of the ways you would like to connect with me when you are busy? If I need to contact you quickly, what are the best times for me to reach you via phone?
Conversing	• Recap various conversation elements. • Clarify meaning of what something meant. • Find meanings for observed nonverbals.	When we talked, I thought you said you wanted to get together again in person to chat next week. Is that right? You just said you would be going on vacation next week. Does that mean you don't want to have any communication from me until you return to work? Just now I observed a frown on your face. Can you tell me what you are thinking?
Envisioning	• Choose "best" ways to capture the developing vision. • Develop key words or branding statements for partnership work. • Get feedback about a particular visual for some part of partnership work.	Wow! These are some great outcomes for our work. Should we try to get it down in words, pictures, or what? Having a slogan or tagline to use on our external communication would be great. Your thoughts? I really like the logo the students developed for our project. How much do you think it communicates what we are all about?

(Continues)

Table 4.3 (*Continued*)

Collaborative Communication Framework Element	Some Metacommunication Uses	Examples
Committing	• Determine ways to remember commitment decisions. • Check interpersonal commitment needs and how to meet them. • Talk about the kinds of trust that matter now.	What do you think would be a good way to recall our commitments to each other down the road? Would you feel more secure in our partnership if you had more information about the budget? Or is something else needed? Right now, I think it's really important that we know more about each other's capabilities so we can rely on each other to do certain things.
Partner Patterns	• Recognize emerging partner patterns that create a shared identity. • Celebrate the unique features of this particular partnership.	We have developed some unique themes in our work together that help define "us." We need to celebrate the second year of the Healthy Lifestyles Camp. How can we share this milestone best?

and the Third Street Community Center. Sered's statement drills down to the most personal aspects of being involved in community-focused change. Partners need to have or to build trust in order to offset what she calls *vulnerability* and others call *risk*.

Commitment and Trust-Building

Consultants Reina and Reina (2006) have used their education and experiences working with 100 organizations to develop the Reina trust and betrayal model. Recognizing that communication and trust are closely linked (p. 34), they point out that trust-building is reciprocal and continues over time (p. 10), such as throughout the life of a partnership.

Similarly, Vangen and Huxham (2003) identified a "trust building loop" for collaborations between organizations and point out that trust-building is cyclical and requires continuous nurturing (pp. 26–27). Their trust-building loop starts by aiming for realistic outcomes; resulting actions (hopefully) will reinforce trusting attitudes that set the stage to aim for more ambitious collaborative efforts and so on (p. 12).

As an example of some ways that trust-building can work, Dianna spent every Saturday while in high school working with the local Literacy Foundation, helping new immigrants learn to speak English and meet the challenges of daily life in their new home. When Dianna went to college, she wanted to continue that work and called the local Literacy Volunteers agency to inquire about possibilities.

But when she called, Charles, the Literacy Foundation director, told her all new volunteers were required to participate in two days of training prior to working with individuals or families. Dianna's prior experiences did not substitute for this requirement. During the training, it became clear to Charles that Dianna could be trusted. She had a wealth of experience and cared deeply about the people the agency served. So he called on Dianna repeatedly to share past experiences.

By the end of the training, Charles asked Dianna to help plan future trainings. His trust in her was further reinforced when she did a great job. Eventually, Charles offered her a part-time position; he now knew he could count on her!

Interestingly enough, the Reina and Reina (2006) model identifies three distinct types of trust: contractual trust, communication trust, and competence trust. *Contractual trust* works to develop "a mutual understanding that people in the relationship will do what they say they will do" (p. 16). This is part of what Charles experienced with Dianna.

Community engagement partners often develop contractual trust at an organizational level by setting up an MOU. A good MOU establishes guidelines for the important contractual trust behaviors listed by Reina and Reina: manage expectations, establish boundaries, delegate (and determine who will be involved), encourage mutual serving intentions, keep agreements (and spell out what those agreements are), and be consistent.

Reina and Reina (2006) label the next type of trust as *communication trust*; this type has to do with whether or not there is a "willingness to disclose." Behaviors that reflect this variety of trust include sharing information, telling the truth, admitting mistakes, giving and receiving constructive feedback, maintaining confidentiality, and speaking with "good purpose" (i.e., conversing directly with persons with whom there are issues rather than gossiping or unfairly criticizing them behind their backs) (p. 35).

Communication trust enhances each partner's credibility by creating the sense that everybody has something useful to share that benefits the partnership. Ideally, communicators will remain able to talk freely for the most part about items of importance to the partnership or about the partnership work.

Notably, Reina and Reina (2006) point out that the amount of disclosure between people tends to be linked to the level of trust that has been achieved. Sharing everything is not a good thing, though! Nonsupportive responses to disclosures can undermine intimacy (McCornack, 2013, p. 63) or closeness between partners. Also, relationships can be damaged when one partner shares information that the other finds inappropriate or perplexing (Planalp & Honeycutt, 1985). Finally, cultures differ in the ways they self-disclose. Some cultures don't see disclosure as key to becoming closer (McCornack, 2013, p. 64). So monitoring the level and amount of disclosure is a best practice for partners. Link disclosures to information needed by the partner or the partnership for best results.

Also, partners can metacommunicate to let each other know they are willing to share more—for example, "I can tell you more about this situation later if that would help. Right now, let's continue with what we were discussing. Does that work for you?"

Another type of trust identified by Reina and Reina (2006) is *competence trust*, a "trust of capability" (p. 58). In other words, a partner might make a quick judgment about whether the other has the experience or expertise to understand what he was conveying. When Linner worked with faculty and students to design building modifications, she quickly trusted they had the expertise needed. They, in turn, soon trusted that Linner had far more experience with her clients, their needs, and the agency's work.

Specific communication behaviors that reflect that a partner is capable and has the expertise or can gain other capacities needed include acknowledging people's skills and abilities, allowing people to make decisions, involving others and seeking their input, and helping people learn new skills (or investing in them).

In sum, trust builds over time between partners and between organizations. Still, there are times when trust can be damaged, sometimes necessitating repair work (see information about trust betrayal in Reina & Reina, 2006).

Collaborating Practices: Recognize Messiness and Do Repair Work

Despite our best intentions and even with a broad repertoire of knowledge and skills, communication can be messy! We are human and imperfect. So sometimes we say things that we don't really mean or that are unintentionally offensive or hurtful. Or sometimes what we share is not well understood. Saying the wrong thing or failing to create understanding can happen due to differences between people in backgrounds, expertise, worldviews, word usage, and so on. Sometimes, as noted previously, our communication practices can harm the trust we have in one another.

When communication damages a relationship, repair work may be required to reestablish a positive relational climate and positive regard for both partners so that the partnership can move forward. Sometimes this repair work involves metacommunication. But sometimes partners may violate one another in such a way that the other partner no longer wants to continue. This kind of situation may require professional conflict intervention for partners to continue working toward positive community outcomes. Other times, a quick "I'm sorry" when trust is violated will be enough to warrant another chance to work together.

Regardless, communication is central to the effective management of differences. Often, repair work shows that one or both partners need to grow in some way. That change could well involve adding more skills and practices to one's communication repertoire.

Worth the Learning and Effort

Learning new ways to positively communicate and build effective, well-functioning partnerships is complex and ongoing. One never fully arrives. But partners can watch for little successes (or big ones!) and celebrate these wins along the way. Partners who recognize and communicate about partnership successes can provide reassurance that the relationship is built on solid ground for future efforts. That's a great place to be!

Spotlight: Seattle University–Bailey Gatzert School Partnership Story

Children walk single file down a hall adorned with brightly colored artwork. Some are in burkas while others wear T-shirts and jeans, but all talk quietly, smiling as they follow the teacher. This memorable scene is an everyday occurrence that adds to the rich educational experiences at Bailey Gatzert Elementary School (Bailey Gatzert) in Seattle, Washington. This school embraces multiple cultures and ethnicities: 46% of the students are Black, 23% are Hispanic, 21% are Asian or Pacific Islander, 4% are two or more races, and 4% are White, with the remainder listed as American Indian/Alaska Native or Hawaiian Native/Pacific Islander (Great! Schools, n.d.).

Bailey Gatzert has long been recognized as the Seattle school with the highest percentage of free and reduced price lunches. Still, the learning trajectory for children attending this school has changed from low grades and diminished futures to an environment where most thrive. Two hours have been added to the school day, which "contribute 35,000 hours of additional learning time (almost 20 percent more time per student, per year)" (Seattle University Youth Initiative, n.d.-b). This transition is due, in large part, to a sustained partnership between Seattle University and the elementary school.

"The Youth Initiative's intended impact is to create a pipeline of support for youth and families living in the low-income neighborhood adjacent to campus and to deepen SU [Seattle University] student learning and understanding of inequities," says Sally Haber, associate director of K–12 partnerships at the Center for Service and Community Engagement. Haber is responsible for the day-to-day management of this partnership.

The Seattle University Youth Initiative program started in February of 2011 and has won multiple national awards. It was listed by *U.S. News & World Report* in its article on the best service-learning schools. It has also received the President's Higher Education Service Award. (See Seattle University Youth Initiative, n.d.-a, for more information about these awards.)

The Extended Learning Program (ELP) after school is the cornerstone of the core services that Seattle University provides at Bailey Gatzert. Currently, over 150 K through 5 students participate in the ELP, with support from 90 students, comprising a mix of volunteers and student employees. They facilitate reading, writing, math, technology, and science learning activities. In addition to academic support, Bailey Gatzert's second through fifth graders participate in enrichment activities that include arts, music, and sports. The ELP at Bailey Gatzert has given university students a chance to help the children focus more on science, an area that needed more attention. With the extra time "in 2012–13, 55 percent of [Bailey] Gatzert fifth graders passed the State MSP Science test (up from 10 percent in 2010–11)," according to the Seattle University Youth Initiative 2012–13 Annual Report (n.d.-a, p. 3).

This community-campus partnership flourishes due to successful communication. According to Kent Koth, director of the Center for Service and Community Engagement at Seattle University, "It is communication that needs to occur at multiple levels."

Greg Imel, principal of Bailey Gatzert, says, "A good trustful relationship needs to be developed so that the communication that does happen is transparent but is ongoing." Both sides of the partnership believe wholeheartedly in relationship-building in order for a partnership to work. Koth adds, "Relationships are essential, and that is the listening and trust. . . . It is about the human relationships." Haber reiterates, "The people and the relationships and the care that we have for each other also has really contributed to our success."

By choice, Bailey Gatzert Elementary School is the driver in decision-making for the partnership. This approach yields success. Unlike other partnerships that focus on the university, this one builds on what Bailey Gatzert wants and needs. Sometimes this requires Seattle University to choose among options that others outside the school might want or even prefer. According to Koth, "One of the roles we [Seattle University] play here is we are the mediator in terms of the communication of needs and opportunities and exploration [at Bailey Gatzert]. We are in constant conversation with how we can be of assistance and how the students can learn."

Koth says the university learned early on that "another lesson is the balance between the campus needs and resources, and the community's needs and their resources, and to make sure we're doing our best to match."

Although the partnership has been successful, there is always room for improvement. "The challenge of power dynamics, race, class, and national origin in terms of residents we are working with" is an ongoing challenge according to Koth. But everyone concerned is willing to address those issues to benefit the children and the families in the school's neighborhood, and to take the lead on showing that the goals of the school are the primary focus.

Whereas many other community-campus partnerships focus on growth and expansion, this intensive partnership began in 2011 and is now focused on stability and refining what is already well under way. Principal Imel says, "More is not necessarily better and what we are doing is very strong and I want to make it sustainable. I do not want to just keep adding, adding, and adding."

Author's Note: Not long ago, Shelby Hackney, a junior active with the Seattle Youth Initiative, worked with others on campus to create the inaugural Bailey Gatzert Game Day. Families from the elementary school came to campus for a day of games, scavenger hunts, and performances to learn about living active lifestyles. Hackney explained her vision: "The intention of having SU [Seattle University] mentors help Bailey Gatzert students understand the fun and importance of living active lifestyles while inviting them and their families to our campus . . . (means) the Bailey Gatzert–Seattle U bond will be strengthened."

Putting Chapter Ideas Into Action

Action for Partnerships and Teaching About Partnerships

1. In class with students or in a workshop with community partners (or with a combination), practice using the various steps of supportive communication in some skits that the group has brainstormed or set up in advance. Getting familiar with a new set of steps in a safe setting helps in the future when using them "in the field."
2. Create opportunities to practice meaning-clarifying practices. Perception checking, paraphrasing, and metacommunication are practices that can feel awkward initially but can pay off in terms of mutual understanding. Have several case studies available so students or partners can use them to practice the three communication practices described in the chapter.

Action for Community-Engaged Scholarship

1. Bronfenbrenner (2009) developed a widely used theory of family systems. He argued that people develop within "nested structures, each one inside the next, like a set of Russian dolls" (p. 3). In community engagement, relational or partnership communication is embedded within nested groups representing systems of communication at other levels. This idea is potentially useful to scholars as they sort out various lines of communication that may travel both within and across systems (or boundaries). Potentially, systems can be mapped visually to see what is working and what might need to be changed in ways similar to asset mapping. Such visuals could yield valuable insights into the present and the future of partnerships. Identifying communication within

different nested areas or within the whole system could also be useful in shedding light on what impacts the partnership. Internal and external communication-related practices and policies might then be targeted in future institutional efforts to partner with the intended community(ies).

2. Boundary spanning is a valuable topic in community engagement because campuses and communities represent "different worlds," as noted by Sandy and Holland (2006). Scholars may want to look at how "permeable" various communication boundaries may be. Interestingly, Siegel (2010) argues that boundaries are becoming more permeable in terms of sharing information with diverse others. He says this creates the need for ongoing negotiation about partnership identities and activities. In addition, Heath and Frey (2004) point out that community collaboration is blurring boundaries between organizations and society. Related research questions might include the following: What do these conceptualizations mean for scholarship about boundary-spanning communication? What kinds of methods or techniques do we need to use to study the varied contexts where communication may be involved in our community-engaged partnerships? Plenty of additional questions could be added to this burgeoning area, with enlightening foci coming from different disciplines.

3. Dumlao and Janke (2012) detail how relational dialectics and dialectical tensions work in community engagement. In short, dialectical tensions are ongoing, natural, and normal parts of relationship dynamics, and not totally resolvable. Dialectical tensions provide potentially useful information for partners as they navigate different aspects of their partnership and their work together. More research about dialectical tensions could be important to learning about what makes partnerships sustainable (or not).

5

LEADERSHIP IN A CHANGING WORLD

*We must not, in trying to think about how we can make a big difference,
ignore the small daily differences we can make which, over time, add
up to the big differences that we often cannot foresee.*

—Marian Wright Edelman

Opportunities to practice leadership exist for all of us. We don't have to have an administrative position to make a positive impact in our world (Astin & Astin, 2000; Komives, Wagner, & Associates, 2009; Schmitz, 2012).

Remember the student who worked collaboratively with others to build a playground? That student leveraged the efforts of many from the community and from the campus to create a new park that would benefit community children and families for years to come. That student showed leadership in action. You can do something similar based on your own interests and passions whether you are a student or a staff, faculty, or community member.

Paul Schmitz (2012), founder and former CEO of the Public Allies program, put it like this: "Leadership is an action many can take, not a position few can hold" (p. 13). Everyone leads by taking personal and social responsibility to engage with diverse campus and community members in order to work together toward common goals (p. xviii). (Visit publicallies.org for more about Public Allies.)

Today's leaders are influenced by diversity and differences, rapid inflow of information from multiple sources, global changes that alter markets, increasing public opinions about organizations and their activities (Hersted & Gergen, 2013, pp. 23–24) and more. Showing leadership is both challenging and rewarding. Leaders skilled at building relationships, engaging in multiperspective reflection (Hersted & Gergen, 2013, p. 24), influencing diverse others, and responding positively to change can become persuasive, powerful, and valuable to communities.

About This Chapter

This chapter focuses on promising leadership knowledge and practices that align with the community engagement ideals of reciprocity, mutual benefit, and shared power. This chapter also links leadership practices back to the collaborative communication model presented in chapter 3.

Leadership, in this sense, is about inspiring and encouraging others to complete a task, develop a project or program, or transform a community. These leaders use power and influence in ways that benefit all, not just a select few. They foster effective relationships and work well together. They are skilled communicators/listeners who have strong values focused on what's good for all of us.

This chapter does not cover all writings about leaders and leadership; it purposely omits the unethical, coercive approaches used by some leaders. Coercion involves using tactics and communication that force or intimidate others, often asking them to do something against their will. Johnson (2001) explains how "the power that comes from being a leader can be used for evil as well as for good. When we assume . . . leadership, we also assume ethical burdens" (p. 4).

The collaborative communication framework embraces positive transformation. Leaders skilled in collaborative communication tend to promote unity rather than division, contribute with others rather than coerce them, and promote teamwork rather than emphasize group differences. The overriding goal, then, is to build cohesive, responsive communities where people genuinely care about one another and work together, ably responding to differences and challenges so that real change happens for all.

University-Based Power: Guiding Principles

Community members tend to see universities and colleges as a means to secure resources such as money, expertise, and students, the kinds of power that many community groups may lack. Interestingly enough, administrator Byron White (2015), now vice president of Knowledge Works Foundation and executive director of Strive Partnership, offers three guiding principles for those from campus working with community members.

1. Motive is more important than outcome. It's important to be transparent about what's in it for those from the universities when we explain "why" we do what we do. If we don't share this information, others in the community will invent it.
2. Authority is earned, not granted. Each of us needs to be able to explain what we have done for this community. Authority is gained by *care*, not by technical expertise.
3. Do not seek goodwill, comfort, or that cozy all-is-well feeling. "These warm fuzzies will not sustain our work with communities. We need to have the tensions to move us forward, while also recognizing that relationships are fragile."

White's apt guidance offers university-based partners like students, faculty, administrators, and staff important ground rules to use when working collaboratively with community partners. Truth is, this is good advice *any* time we seek to work in harmony with others.

Definitions of *Power*

Leaders sometimes focus on power as control over other people (i.e., coercive or dictatorial), but other ways to think about power promote positive community change. For instance, Hackman and Johnson (2009) define *power* as "the ability to influence others . . . in order to modify attitudes and/or behaviors" (p. 136). Power, they say, is the "currency of leadership" (p. 137) and involves skillful listening and collaborative-style communication.

Interestingly enough, French and Raven (1959) long ago identified six power bases (coercive, reward, legitimate, expert, referent, and information) that are still relevant today. The last three listed—expert, referent, and information—have been termed *soft powers* that give everyone, not just a single leader, freedom and autonomy (Pierro, Raven, Amato, & Bérlanger, 2013). These soft powers are highly relevant to community engagement.

With expert power, the first soft power, influence comes through supplying needed information and related professional skills to others (Hackman & Johnson, 2009, p. 141). One example of expert power would be a scholar knowledgeable about community nutrition because of her academic training, research, and teaching responsibilities. This nutrition scholar could share needed information with community members regarding nutrient-dense foods and meal preparation techniques that promote better health. This kind of influence (or power) holds the possibility of changing eating patterns.

Another example of expert power would be a community partner who specializes in working with homeless populations. He could speak knowledgeably about needs, constraints, and other concerns that homeless community members face every day. The information shared would be invaluable to campus members working in a community shelter or planning projects of mutual benefit with homeless individuals and families.

A second soft power, referent power, involves role modeling, where admirers give their role model the power to influence their behavior. For instance, a community leader who garners the respect of people from different social and ethnic groups could rally them to actively create a more prosperous neighborhood in a formerly distressed area. Or a campus leader everybody trusts and sees as influential could encourage others to address local environmental issues. Changes to a local trash cleanup program might be traced back to the referent power of this campus leader.

There's one major caution here, though. Referent power can break. If the role model's esteem and respect are questioned for some reason, soft power can shatter for this leader. In other words, if the leader is seen as dishonest or untrustworthy or immoral for some action, his or her influence with others can wane or even disappear.

A third soft power is information power. In today's world, sharing information via social media, for instance, can influence many and create a public call to action. A journalism student who writes for the college newspaper has information power to craft stories that influence others. Similarly, the newsletter editor for a community organization has information power to shape ideas for those community members receiving the publication.

Collaborative Communication for Today's Leaders

While power is important, additional communication capabilities are both necessary and useful for today's leaders. Well-honed public speaking, interorganizational, and media usage knowledge and skills are highly valuable to leaders but beyond the scope of this book. Instead, the focus will be on helping leaders foster interpersonal relationships and build a collaborative communication repertoire.

Nitin Nohria says, "Communication is the real work of leadership" (Harvard Business School, 2001). That's true today more than ever! Relational communication, conversations that reflect emotional and social intelligence, group communication skills, persuasive communication abilities, and boundary-spanning capacities are all crucial to leaders in today's world. Let's consider each one.

Relational Communication

Relational communication matters to leaders as they influence others to bring about change. Wood (2007) says five skills are tied to interpersonal (relational) communication competence:

1. Developing a range of communication skills
2. Adapting communication appropriately
3. Engaging in dual-perspective thinking
4. Monitoring communication
5. Committing to effective and ethical communication practices (p. 35)

This entire book focuses on helping you develop a repertoire or range of collaborative communication abilities so you can adapt or be flexible in the moment to make choices that best suit the person(s) and the situation you face. In that way, the entire book supports the first two skills listed by Wood (2007) for developing relational communication competence.

The third skill, engaging dual-perspective thinking, involves the abilities to shift back and forth seamlessly between what you think and feel to what another might think or feel (Phillips & Wood, 1983; see also chapter 3). Having dual perspectives means you can listen, hear, and understand where the other person is coming from and hold that in mind even while you are aware of your own perspectives. This cognitive capacity takes practice but is imperative for combining the "me" and "we" needed for community engagement work.

For instance, Mony was looking out for his business partner, Simary, and representing her at an important community meeting about an upcoming big box store that was potentially going to buy out the local farmland they owned together and used to support campus food programs. Mony and Simary were working to create a sustainable organic farm on the land that would also sell produce through a local food cooperative.

Simary couldn't attend the community meeting because she was taking a Nutrition and Community class on campus that could not be missed. She and Mony had talked in depth about what they both thought about the issues on the agenda. Simary had enlisted her professors to supply data about what the big box store would mean economically for the entire region as well as about what their organic farm might contribute locally, including to the campus. At the meeting, when Mony thought about what to say, he considered his own thoughts and opinions as well as those thoughts and data Simary had shared with him. That way, with her permission, Mony was able to represent them both.

The fourth important relational skill involves monitoring communication as it happens. Monitoring communication involves attending to your own verbal and nonverbal actions to see how your communication impacts others. Monitoring communication does not mean making judgments about yourself or the other person. Rather, monitoring involves self-awareness of the communication elements you are using so you can actively respond in the moment rather than react emotionally or without thinking.

Keep in mind the distinction between responding (with choice) rather than reacting emotionally (without thought) as you consider the example of Jamie, a student leader, who noticed that she was having some difficulty communicating well with Juan, a member of the community she had partnered with to build a long-term volunteer program with her sorority. Something told her that they didn't always really connect or understand one another. So each time she talked with him now she carefully listened and watched his responses to each word and action. Because of this communication monitoring, Jamie made some important observations. Juan seemed to react with a puzzled look on his face whenever she used idioms. (Idioms are groups of words or expressions that have meaning not readily apparent from the words themselves.)

One day when they talked, Jamie said she was "tickled pink" and then saw Juan's puzzled facial expression as part of his reaction. So she asked Juan directly, "Do you know what 'tickled pink' means?" He shook his head no. She explained that she was really happy and excited with what had happened—that she was "tickled pink." Juan smiled widely and grabbed a little notebook he kept in his pocket and jotted down some words.

From that day on, Juan came to Jamie to ask about unusual expressions or idioms he'd heard to see if she could explain them. She did. What started as Jamie's self-monitoring turned out to be an important and functional way that Jamie and Juan interacted. Both of them enjoyed this special aspect of their relationship with one another and it became a partner pattern between them.

The fifth relational communication capacity, committing to ethical communication practices, is a vital part of working with a community partner. Ethics have to do with moral judgments about what is "right" or "wrong," "good" or "bad," and communicating in alignment with those judgments or values. The National Communication Association (n.d.), a large professional communication organization, says ethical behavior is guided by values like integrity, fairness, professional and social responsibility, equality of opportunity, confidentiality, honesty and openness, respect for self and others, freedom, and safety. These values are well aligned with community engagement best practices as well. It all sounds easy, but ethical communication is not always simple in practice.

For instance, personal values and community or social values can conflict, making ethical communication choices muddy. Consider Rosita, who wanted to participate in her class project to build a Habitat for Humanity house on an upcoming Saturday. The expectation of her group members was that she would come that day because she had been involved in all the preparatory planning. Further, a major portion of their course grade depended on having all group members present and actively involved that day.

Rosita's family expected her to fully participate in her grandmother's ninetieth birthday party that very same day. Relatives from out of town were coming to celebrate. There would be food, music, and fun. Moreover, letting her family and grandma down by not being there all day long would be a major insult to her family and would have long-term consequences culturally.

Rosita decided to talk to the professor to see if there was any way to do additional coursework to benefit her group and their joint grade. Luckily, the professor understood. They decided together that Rosita would lead efforts to fund and prepare a class gift for the new homeowners. This innovative response allowed Rosita to complete her class (i.e., professional responsibilities) and also to attend the important family event (i.e., social responsibilities).

Ethical communication, like other kinds of communication, takes practice and involves lifelong learning as people, communication technology, and situations change. Often, ethical decision-making requires thinking about the emotional and social implications of various actions.

Emotional and Social Intelligences for Today's Leaders

A leader's well-honed abilities to use emotional and social intelligences wisely are paramount in community engagement work. "Emotional intelligence enables leaders to deal with their own internal responses, moods, and states of mind. Social intelligence informs how we understand and interact with others" (McKee, Boyatzis, & Johnston, 2008, p. 25).

Individuals with emotional and social intelligences tend to (a) be aware of their own feelings, (b) deal with their own emotions constructively, (c) harness emotions in ways that promote decision-making and relational problem-solving communication (Kotze & Venter, 2011), (d) listen to their own feelings and those of others to learn from them (Wood, 2007, p. 187), (e) take the perspective of another person and show empathy for that person, and (f) have a strong yet realistic sense of optimism (Wood, 2007, p. 187).

Considering emotional and social intelligences in depth is beyond the scope of this book. Still, cultivating these intelligences can add to one's collaborative communication repertoire and greatly facilitate leadership capabilities. (See also the resources in the appendix and bibliography.)

Group Influence and Audience Analysis

Whether working with a small group, giving a community presentation, or using media, leadership involves getting others engaged in change-making by sharing important concepts or visions. Listeners will more likely act on concepts or visions presented if you, as leader, connect deeply with them. Otherwise, those listening are likely to feel like you "missed the mark" because your sharing didn't line up with their needs, interests, or ways of learning. So you can increase your effectiveness in sharing exponentially if you do some audience analysis first.

Audience analysis involves figuring out what information matters most to the other person or group and what channels might be most effective for sharing that content. Audience analysis helps you choose language and organize message elements, too. One way of thinking about this quickly is to use the memory device RPPF for reader, purpose, publication, focus. (*Note*: The basic idea can be adapted for both written and spoken presentations. See Table 5.1 for more details.)

Consider, for example, RPPF with a community-based project. Robyn was the director of a local health department in a community that needed to address the prominence of high blood pressure, a "silent killer" that could significantly increase risks of heart disease and stroke (Centers for Disease Control, 2018). She also knew that "about 1 out of 3 U.S. adults—or about 70 million people—have high blood pressure. Only about half (52%) of these people have their blood pressure under control" (Centers for Disease Control, 2018).

So as she began to plan for a local health fair and set up goals for the coming year, she reached out to Dr. Takata, a local expert on the topic. When they met and talked over coffee, Dr. Takata invited her to attend the health fair with a few students and then asked Robyn if they could do a community-based project together. Robyn enthusiastically agreed and they talked about ways to help the students learn and to make the project valuable to the community members and to her.

Dr. Takata explained that the students knew a lot of details about the links between high blood pressure, heart disease, and stroke. But the students didn't know the community very well. She set up a time for Robyn to come to the class to relate her experiences. After sharing, Robyn asked the students to develop new materials for the community that could be shared at a Community Health Day she was planning several months later.

TABLE 5.1
Audience Analysis Worksheet

Analysis Factors	Key Question	Additional Details	Why It Matters
a. Written Documents—Use RPPF to get started			
Reader	What specific group of readers do you want to reach? What content will they need or want?	• Gender • Professional or personal role (what do they need to know?) • Cultural background • Language • And more . . .	Helps choose content, language, style of writing, and related elements for better "fit" to be more relevant and credible with specific readers.
Purpose	What do you want this communication to accomplish?	• To educate/inform • To persuade • To entertain • To publicize • To call to action • Other? Specify.	Strategies exist for sharing information with each of these purposes. Also, purpose shapes content and approach in documents.
Publication	What kind of publication will you use for this communication?	• Magazine • Newspaper • Research paper • Newsletter article • Other? Specify.	Different publications have different formats and styles. Need to match those.
Focus	What is the key idea for your document?	Write a one-sentence summary of the main ideas for your document to keep it focused.	This helps the writer choose content and do targeted research to fit the intended focus.

(Continues)

TABLE 5.1 (*Continued*)

Analysis Factors	Key Question	Additional Details	Why It Matters
b. Presentations—Use APCI to get started			
Audience	What specific group of audience members do you want to reach? What content will they need or want?	• Audience member characteristics (diversity, similarity) • Whether audience is friendly or hostile • Other?	Helps choose content, language, and presentation style for better "fit" to be more relevant and credible with intended audience.
Purpose	What do you want to have people think or do after your presentation?	• To inform/educate • To persuade • To entertain • To call to action • To publicize • Other?	Strategies exist for sharing information with each of these purposes. Also, purpose shapes content and approach in the presentation.
Context/ Setting	Where will you give the presentation? What are the specific features of the setting?	• Conference room • Auditorium • Outdoor setting • Classroom • Other?	Settings and context help determine what equipment or room features will be available to use. (Go early to prepare and practice in the space.)
Key Idea	What is your main idea to share?	Write a one-sentence summary or slogan for your presentation to keep it focused.	This helps the presenter choose content and do targeted research to fit the intended focus.

Robyn helped the students meet a group of women who really enjoyed cooking together. The students decided to work with this team of cooks to develop some healthy but tasty recipes. The students were also introduced to some local storytellers. The students collaborated with these storytellers to create several stories about blood pressure tailored specifically to people in the local community.

After meeting with the cooks and storytellers (*reader*/audience) the students crafted their specific *purpose* statement: to share information that was both educational *and* practical. Next they determined the *publication*/ presentation for sharing—use recipes and stories at the Community Health Day presentation and in a brochure they could leave with those attending. Their intended *focus* in the presentation and brochure was details about blood pressure, related health risks, and specific steps for community members to try new recipes and change lifestyle patterns.

The students learned firsthand from the cooks and storytellers about the importance of connecting with community members in order to share information well. This approach promised better possibilities for change than the purely academic fact-sharing they might have tried before doing community-based audience analysis.

Persuasion and Influence

Most leaders use influence to bring about change through persuasion—to get others to think or act differently. Once you've gathered the RPPF data, you can think about whether you intend to appeal to the head, the heart, or the hands (or some combination). Appeals to the head involve thinking processes. Appeals to the heart relate to emotions. Appeals to the hands concern taking action. Or you can combine appeals.

For instance, by choosing words that influence the thoughts of another, it is possible to reinforce ideas or change patterns of thinking. Influencing someone with a similar view requires a thorough, well-researched case and support for each point. But when the person's views are widely different from your own, the leader/influencer must effectively counter each objection that could be raised. That can be challenging and to work well involves really knowing the reader/audience.

Suppose you were trying to convince a friend to use sunscreen to avoid skin cancer. Your prior conversations indicated that he didn't think slapping on SPF lotion mattered for him. Only fair-skinned people or children needed sunscreen, to his way of thinking. Several steps would be needed to persuade your friend to think differently. Information about the value of sunscreens would be necessary as well as details about the consequences for everybody of not using sunscreens. Any objections he might have about using sunscreens would be important to anticipate and counter, too. By following these steps well, you would stand a chance of convincing him to try sunscreen. But making additional appeals to the heart (emotional examples) and also to the hands might be even more effective.

Appeals to the heart awaken emotions in the other person. This is one way emotional intelligence can benefit a leader—by being emotionally savvy and able to use emotional control to appeal to the feelings of others in an ethical fashion. Whereas head appeals rely heavily on logic and well-supported arguments, heart appeals rely on nonverbals and words that elicit an inner stirring or heartfelt reaction.

Think for a minute about some of the commercials on television that show abused animals. The content includes limited factual information, but the pictures, the background music, and the tone of the spoken words are geared toward arousing emotions. The commentary also focuses on the need to contribute financially to prevent future animal abuse. Although some head appeals are made (i.e., to contribute and to get involved), most of these commercials rely on heart appeals (i.e., to get an emotional response). Then, after reeling in viewers emotionally, the commercials ask viewers to take action.

Appeals to the hands require action. We've all heard people say, "I just had to do something rather than sit around and think about it." So an effort to secure immediate donations of food, clothing, and other supplies to send to flood victims quickly would likely use an appeal to the hands by urging quick action.

Regardless of whether your persuasive efforts as a leader focus on appeals to the head, to the heart, or to the hands, learning to work ethically and effectively across differences can prove powerful. Boundary-spanning practices can help with this.

Boundary Spanning and Leadership

The effort "to span physical, relational, psychological, structural, and cultural boundaries" (Dumlao & Janke, 2012, p. 152) is essential to community engagement work (see also Hayes & Cuban, 1997; Janke, 2008). People on campuses and in communities come from "different worlds" (Sandy & Holland, 2006) that need to be bridged so individuals can work together effectively.

In today's rapidly changing world, boundary-spanning practices matter to leaders in varied settings. Importantly, Ernst and Chrobot-Mason (2011) identified six sequential boundary-spanning practices learned by working with businesses in different countries: buffering, reflecting, connecting, mobilizing, weaving, and transforming. They say these practices allow greater agility and flexibility in working together (p. 4) and can help groups "realize more together than they could achieve on their own" (p. 12).

The first step, buffering, helps people "define boundaries and create safety between groups" (p. 9). In community engagement, buffering could involve conversations between people from the campus and community to become clearer about what is "off limits" and what information and ideas can be readily shared. Buffering conversations could also involve disclosing information about "what's in it" for each person (and their organization) as they begin to work together.

For example, Andi was honest in sharing her need to complete a class assignment when she went to the Habitat for Humanity resale shop. In return, the shop's director pointed out that Andi could earn the hours needed, but she would need to do a job that required little training. In this case, they both shared "what's in it" as a buffer to help them work together.

The second step, reflecting, requires in-depth "understanding (of) boundaries to foster respect" (Ernst & Chrobot-Mason, 2011, p. 9). In this step, conversations would focus on learning more about specific differences among the individuals and groups involved.

Think back to the example of Shannon's desire to have a face-to-face conversation when Rachel wanted to use Skype. As they talked about (reflected on) their differences, they better understood the reasons and nuances behind their desired ways to communicate. *Reflecting conversations*, as defined here, often pinpoint reasons behind differences to help community-engaged partners understand one another better.

The third step, connecting, involves "suspending boundaries to build trust between groups" (Ernst & Chrobot-Mason, 2011, p. 10). In these authors' conceptualization, connecting is seen as a way to discover common ground and build togetherness by emphasizing commonalities. Sarah and Aaron connected in terms of commonalities when they learned that they both had a love of Lab dogs. (Notably, this example also helped in building rapport, closeness, and interdependence in the relationship, reflecting the extended definition of *connecting* used in this book as part of the collaborative communication framework.)

Mobilizing, the fourth step for boundary spanning, requires "reframing boundaries to develop intergroup community" (Ernst & Chrobot-Mason, 2011, p. 10). When working with a community partner, this happens when you no longer think about your work as "me" and "you" working together but instead begin to relate to "our work" and "us." Rather than having totally separate identities, you have a joint identity at least part of the time (see Janke, 2008, 2009; also see chapter 3 about partner patterns).

The fifth step, "weaving, occurs when group boundaries 'interlace' (or overlap) yet remain distinct" (Ernst & Chrobot-Mason, 2011, p. 178). Weaving with your community partner involves figuring out how you will work together so that you can rely on one another and really count on each other over time. Interdependence means that you can't do things alone anymore. Instead, you have to come up with the means to work together more effectively despite the individual organizations or groups you represent. You work as a partnership team at times while retaining your separate identities, roles, and functions at other times.

The sixth step, transforming, "cross-cuts boundaries" to enable partners to "work together in new directions to realize emergent possibilities" (Ernst & Chrobot-Mason, 2011, p. 11). True collaborating is needed to do this. This kind of transforming happens when partners actively use *all* elements in the collaborative communication framework in order to build lasting changes for the community when working together. (Several good examples of partnership teams and lasting community changes can be found in the Spotlight stories in this book.)

Social Change and Leadership

The social change model of leadership development created by Komives and colleagues (2009) offers six important principles for those who aspire to transform communities through community engagement work.

1. Leadership is concerned with effecting change on behalf of others and society.
2. Leadership is collaborative.
3. Leadership is a process rather than a position.
4. Leadership should be value-based.
5. All students (not just those who hold formal leadership positions) are potential leaders.
6. Service is a powerful vehicle for developing students' leadership skills. (p. xii)

Please note: While Komives and colleagues (2009) write specifically about students in their book, the ideas shared here also could apply to other campus and community leaders involved in community engagement.

Social change leadership involves seven values: citizenship, common purpose, collaboration, addressing controversy with civility, consciousness of self, congruence, and commitment. Citizenship involves active involvement with the community to promote change that benefits others (p. 54). Common purpose means shared responsibility toward collective aims, values, and visions (p. 54). Collaboration capitalizes on diversity and strengths of the relationships and individuals involved (p. 54). Addressing controversy with civility refers to open, critical yet civil discourse that integrates multiple perspectives, potentially bringing creative new solutions to light (p. 54). Consciousness of self requires awareness of personal beliefs, values, attitudes, and emotions so individuals can be continually reflective and mindful during interactions with others in the group (i.e., use monitoring communication). Congruence is reflected by the integrity and authenticity shown by acting consistently with one's thoughts, values, and beliefs. In other words, a congruent individual "walks the talk" (p. 54). Finally, "commitment requires an intrinsic passion, energy, and purposeful investment toward action" (p. 54) that promotes ongoing individual follow-through and willing involvement to create change.

The six principles are a quick list that recaps key ideas found elsewhere in this book. Each of the values listed provides useful concepts to keep in mind when "doing" collaborative communication as a leader working with others.

Final Thoughts on Community-Engaged Leadership

Multiple challenges facing today's leaders require a broad array of communication practices and processes for success. Increasingly, new technology as well as political and social changes impact the ways that "information can flow—laterally, diagonally, and in spirals," which can disrupt organizations. Indeed, new communication channels are changing long-standing practices and diffusing the distribution of power based on "who knows what" (Ruderman, 2011, p. xv).

Understanding and using innovative approaches to change will be essential to community-engaged leaders. Also, today's leaders will "need to understand how to work in all directions and with all people regardless of occupation, level, location, ancestry, nationality, religion, or . . . other characteristics and beliefs" (Ruderman, 2011, p. xvi). You can use your community-focused service-learning, engaged scholarship, and extended volunteering experiences to learn about and practice leadership. This learning matters in the community, in the classroom, and in today's complex world as we develop new capacities to put collaborative communication into action to effect positive change with others!

Putting Chapter Ideas Into Action

Action for Partnerships and Teaching About Partnerships

1. Leadership development requires attention by all of us if we are to work well together. Have students or community partners identify one or two leadership communication processes or practices that they want to focus

on. The "each one teach one" approach is a good way to share, but it's also a great way to learn (see the appendix and bibliography).

2. With your partner (or with a class) look in depth at one or more social change leadership capabilities. Then have a conversation about topics such as the following: How would this practice work for us? Are there ideas here that seem likely to help us? What ideas listed won't work for us and why? (And what might work instead?) Use the information gleaned from this discussion to put new ideas into practice.

Action for Community-Engaged Scholarship

1. Several leadership concepts in this chapter are new and need to be empirically tested in community-engaged work. The sources listed in the works cited and in the appendix and annotated bibliography give scholars a place to start this exciting work.

2. We know that boundary-spanning processes are important in community engagement. What are some of the ways that boundary spanning can be effective? What are some of the limitations of boundary spanning? Use these exploratory questions to start. Much scholarly work is needed to better understand and cultivate tools for effective boundary spanning in action as we work collaboratively in community-engaged scholarship.

6

NAVIGATING CULTURAL DIFFERENCES WHILE PRESERVING RELATIONSHIPS

Your capacity to connect with diverse people is vital for leading an adventuresome, satisfying life with others and necessary so that you can accomplish something greater together than you can on your own.

—Kare Anderson

As the quote suggests, relating to diverse others creates opportunities for us to learn and grow, as well as to contribute our unique strengths in communities. Together we can create positive changes. We need each other because we *all* have valuable things to share.

The words *culture* and *diversity* provide shorthand for distinctions among people. In this book, *culture* is defined as "learned patterns of behavior and attitudes shared by a group of people" (Martin & Nakayama, 2007, p. 81). These learned patterns originate from national origin, ethnic or racial foundations, family backgrounds, organizational norms, and more.

No matter the source, culture impacts our thinking. Also, "culture is created and maintained through communication" (Humphrey, 2007, pp. 5–7). In fact, culture and communication are so closely interwoven that they are hard to tease apart. Cultural assumptions, practices, and styles of communication become so embedded in our thoughts and behaviors that we consider them part of "who we are."

Diversity Shifts and Impacts on Daily Life

Diversity, in this book, refers to the rich mix of people representing multiple cultural groups. Locally, nationally, and globally, the kinds of people in our lives are changing dramatically, so diversity is a regular part of our lives.

Paul Taylor (2014) from the Pew Research Center draws a vivid picture, saying, "At the same time our [U.S.] population is going gray, we're also becoming multi-colored. In 1960, the population in the United States was 85% white; by 2060, it will be only 43% white. We were once a black and white country. Now we're a rainbow . . . [with] 40 million immigrants who have arrived since 1965, about half of them Hispanics and three-in-ten Asians."

Worldwide, a shift toward a larger percentage of older persons in the population represents an important trend (United Nations Population Division, 2014b). Also, people are increasingly concentrated in cities. By 2050, the world population will be one-third rural and two-thirds urban, reversing trends of the past (United Nations Population Division, 2014a).

In addition, "with rapid changes in the global economy, technology, transportation systems, and immigration policies, the world is becoming a small, intersecting community. No matter where we go, we find ourselves having increased contact with people who are culturally different" (Ting-Toomey & Chung, 2012, p. 5). Learning to communicate well with people from diverse backgrounds is now a necessity. It is important to all of us to find ways to connect, converse, and collaborate.

About This Chapter

One valuable way to think about cultural distinctions in interacting is to use a dialectical approach. Rather than thinking of cultural contrasts with another person as "my way" *or* "your way," a dialectical approach considers "my way" *and* "your way" as occurring together naturally in an intercultural relationship. This chapter will share different dialectical pairs that scholars have identified for intercultural relationships.

This chapter also details other communication patterns used by different cultural groups worldwide. This background provides solid grounding for becoming more aware of cultural specifics. Concepts like relational empathy, authentic listening, and flexible communication can also guide us. The chapter ends with descriptions of how the collaborative communication framework can be applied in cross-cultural partnerships between community and campus members.

Dialectical Framework to Examine Culture and Communication

The notion of dialectics dates back to the ancient Greeks and has been applied to interpersonal relationships (Baxter, 1990; Baxter & Montgomery, 1996) and to relationships between community-campus partners (Dumlao & Janke, 2012), as well as to intercultural communication specifically (Martin & Nakayama, 2007). Dialectics assume that two (or more) seemingly contradictory characteristics work *with* each other, not against one another.

Instead of thinking of differences as opposite perspectives that can't be reconciled, we hold multiple viewpoints in mind simultaneously. (This echoes the idea of dual-perspective thinking found in earlier chapters.) If you locate each part of the dialectical pair on different ends of a continuum or continuous line, you can see that they are related, not entirely separate from one another.

One well-recognized dialectic in all relationships is stability versus change (sometimes called static versus dynamic). For instance, when thinking about how to share information with his community, Max, a health center director, prefers the tried-and-true method of using an e-mail newsletter (i.e., stability) to connect with the community. But Arum, a graduate student volunteer, uses Twitter to get the word out quickly (i.e., change). By thinking about stability versus change as being located on the same continuum, Max and Arum can consider their decisions holistically (Holliday, Hyde, & Kullman, 2010, p. 87). This recognition gives Max and Arum a neutral base for conversations about how to manage their ideas and preferences about how to get the word out to their community.

In addition, each dialectical perspective can have multiple layers that are interrelated. Arum, for example, may understand that Twitter offers speed, wide access, and can be a powerful part of an active social media strategy. His social media knowledge is likely reflected in his conversations with Max about Twitter. Max could, in response, offer examples of how e-mail news works well with members of his community who might want to mull over the information and refer back to it later on. He knows what e-mail newsletters can do. This multilayered knowledge would be reflected in his conversations with Arum.

Somewhat similarly, "different layers of culture can intertwine in complex ways" (Holliday et al., 2010, pp. 5–7). When we communicate with someone representing a different cultural group, the layers of personal background may interact to inform the messages that person sends and receives. For example, Shawanda came from a poor inner city neighborhood populated heavily by Black and Hispanic residents. She grew up thinking that all police were unfair to members of her community and that they expected everybody there to be prone to crime and violence, which she thought was a really unfair line of reasoning. Shawanda knew there were law-abiding citizens in her neighborhood along with a few troublemakers who needed better ways to deal with their frustrations and meet their needs.

So when Shawanda was asked to be part of a group to meet in person with two police officers, she was reluctant to go. Still, her grandmom had always encouraged her to "think the best first; then act accordingly." Because of her grandmom's advice, Shawanda held out some hope that if group members and the police officers could get to know one another as individuals, they might begin to get beyond negative stereotypes. Knowing that a counseling team from campus that was well known and liked in the neighborhood would guide the conversations also helped her decide to attend.

Shawanda spoke hesitatingly at first. But, as she listened to the unexpected thoughtful, caring responses from the officers, she felt more confident to speak candidly. By the end of that meeting she was aware that some positive changes were possible. So Shawanda agreed to work with the others to find new solutions to problems, even while recognizing that long-term change would be challenging.

At the same time, Officer Martha had been asked by her boss to go with her partner to that same meeting in the community. As a rookie officer with limited direct experience with that community, Officer Martha didn't really know what to expect. But she'd heard stories about violence in the neighborhood, so she was a little apprehensive. Still, she followed orders and planned to go with her partner.

At the meeting, Officer Martha found that Shawanda offered thoughtful, eloquent explanations for what life in her community was like. Officer Martha respected Shawanda and listened carefully to what she had to say. Those initial negative ideas began to change and Officer Martha suggested specific ways that she and her partner could build positive relationships with those present as well as with others in the community. New possibilities for working together began to take shape.

Dialectical thinking encourages us to look at ongoing changes in individuals and their cultural groups, to use a process approach to communication. Although unique interactions can happen in one episode of conversation, ingrained patterns of communication reflecting cultural backgrounds will play out in varied ways as partners interrelate over time.

Dialectics in Intercultural Communication

Martin and Nakayama (2007) have identified six dialectics specific to intercultural communication: cultural-individual, personal-contextual, difference-similarity, static-dynamic, history/past-present/future, and privilege-disadvantage. Each of these pairs is described next, followed by an example with community-campus partners.

The cultural-individual dialectic means that communication is not only specific to the individual but also reflects communication patterns of cultural groups to which that person belongs (Martin & Nakamaya, 2007, p. 71). In her interactions with her community partner, Carly, at the local neighborhood center, Mani pointed out that her personal preference was to "say what you mean" and be very direct. She had learned that pattern in school and liked it. But she also recognized that this new communication style contrasted with that of her Asian family members. Her mother and aunts frequently gained the gist of conversations through socially learned nonverbal cues. They believed that words could be deceiving, so nonverbal or contextually based cues tended to get most of their attention.

In advance, Mani told Carly about her own choice to "say what you mean" in contrast to other family members, who would rely heavily on nonverbal cues. Once they adjusted to these differences, everyone was able to work together to develop culturally respectful brochures that encouraged new Asian immigrants to use the neighborhood center's available services.

Another pair, the personal-contextual dialectic, means that although we communicate as individuals on a personal level, the context of communication also matters (Martin & Nakamaya, 2007, p. 71). For instance, Al, the director of a nonprofit organization serving the homeless, was baffled when his university partner, Marina, said current service-learning students could serve meals, but next semester's students would need to attend a lengthy orientation first. Al wasn't used to this contextually based practice. Most other volunteers he knew had worked continually with the community kitchen for years. He asked Marina why the same students couldn't continue their work with him in another service-learning course. Then he wondered why a new course couldn't be added to the curriculum so they could continue working at the kitchen with him. An in-depth conversation with Marina helped Al better understand the personal and contextual factors that impact students' lives and the way the university functions. Together, they came up with ways to help address Al's needs for assistance.

The next pair, the difference-similarity dialectic, recognizes that communication reflects both distinctions and commonalities between people from diverse cultures (Martin & Nakamaya, 2007, p. 72). For instance, Sanya preferred to avoid problems and not discuss differences with her classmates. Her cultural background focused on maintaining harmony even when there are differences; each person would give a little or else one would defer to another rather than create friction.

When it came to doing classwork, though, a frank conversation was clearly what the other students expected from Sanya. They all shared the need to get the course assignment done within a week. So even though this was new and felt awkward, Sanya decided to try their approach to problem-solving. Her classmates discussed the problem gingerly to minimize Sanya's discomfort, focusing as much as possible on identifying common ground. They also determined ways to work together to write down the solution so they could all complete the assignment well in advance of the due date.

The static-dynamic dialectic (similar to stability-change) recognizes that "some cultural and communication patterns remain relatively constant, whereas other aspects of cultures (or traits of individuals) shift over time" (Martin & Nakamaya, 2007, p. 72). When the new Asian immigrants came to the community center for the first time with Mani's relatives, they continued to use their preferred nonverbal and indirect communication practices with one another. During their first conversation with Carly, they hinted at participating in the job-training program. But that approach left everyone confused. So Mani suggested that several community members might come together to the center (respecting their cultural community-focused pattern) while also having a spokesperson ask for various services, such as job training for the whole group. This way of respecting both stable and changing communication patterns worked better for everyone.

The history/past-present/future dialectic reflects that current realities influence communication and that history impacts present events and situations (Martin & Nakamaya, 2007, p. 73) and what content shows up in communication. Cultures vary in time focus. For example, Lealand always considers the history of his district whenever he plans next steps for community economic development. He knows that people in his district focus on a history/past orientation. What happened to them previously matters a lot and is a big part of how they see the world. In contrast, the community development team from campus led by Jason wants to focus on the future.

Gradually, Lealand and Jason's team conversed and came to terms with this dialectic. They decided to incorporate past/present/future perspectives into the vision statement and then build action steps to benefit the community as well as the development team. Everyone wins when they combine the different elements of this dialectical pair.

The privilege-disadvantage dialectic recognizes that "people may be simultaneously privileged and disadvantaged, or privileged in some contexts and disadvantaged in others" (p. 73). Consider Patricia St. Onge and colleagues' (2009) example about culture and nonprofits:

> At one point, I was executive director at a program that served homeless women and their children. Rather than doing the usual intake—asking

them to share their problems—we asked each woman to identify three skills, gifts, or talents she brought into the household. . . . As the women discovered that they did have skills and gifts, their participation changed . . . . They saw themselves as resources for the community rather than needy women taking from the program. (p. 4)

The conversations of St. Onge and the group members took a strengths-based approach to identifying ways that each person could contribute. This effectively addressed the privilege-disadvantage dialectic for them. Continued discussions could provide a way to consider past inequalities and find ways to change those patterns to build stronger, more equitable relationships for the future.

One important caveat: It's tempting to think that all dialectics can be managed by compromising or by changing the situation so the dialectics aren't apparent. But that won't always work! Keep in mind that dialectics are natural and normal in relationships between people. In fact, any particular dialectical pair may ebb and flow in a relationship depending on people and their current circumstances—*but the dialectical pair never completely disappears.*

The real challenge then is to learn ways to converse about dialectically related differences and then to work collaboratively with partners to develop strategies to manage them effectively. Indeed, because dialectical pairs recur, we will likely need to discuss each one more than once as we continue to work together over time.

Cultural Value Patterns and Communication

Other oft-recognized cultural value patterns impact understanding and communication, too. Hofstede (1980, 1991, 2001) surveyed people in more than 50 countries to glean dimensions of cultural variability. He identified five dimensions that influence people's assumptions about the world and also reflect a specific style of communication: individualism-collectivism, power distance variations, feminine-masculine value dimensions, levels of uncertainty avoidance, and short-term or long-term orientation.

Individualism and collectivism have been widely studied (Hofstede, 1980, 2001; Oyserman, Kemmelmeier, & Coon, 2002; Triandis, 1988, 1995). Shearman, Dumlao, and Kagawa (2011) state, "Individualism refers to the degree to which people value individualistic achievements and self-expression. Collectivism, on the other hand, refers to the degree to which people value collectivistic achievement and group harmony" (p. 106). In a collectivistic culture, "one's self is seen as inseparable from those of other in-group members" (p. 106).

As an example, consider Rachel, a designated community leader accustomed to making decisions for her organization solo. Rachel had been selected to lead because of her strong abilities to consider the needs and desires of others. But Kimoto comes from a collectivistic cultural background; his research team always worked together to make decisions about every step of their scholarly work.

As Rachel and Kimoto's collaborative research proceeded, all participants needed to converse, adapt, and determine what they could do as a team. They talked through whether individual initiative or collective efforts might work best. In other words, they coordinated when "we" or "me" would function better for the good of the whole partnership and their intended work.

Power dimensions also vary between cultures. People working in community engagement talk and write about equalizing power in our partnerships. Ideally, we want to have everybody fully involved in all aspects of our collaborative work. Still, cultural variations in power distance impact assumptions about how things get done, as well as the level of deference naturally given to a person of a different status.

For example, Gudykunst (1998) notes, "Individuals from high power distance cultures accept power as part of society" (p. 61) and see status differences as natural and normal. In contrast, "In small power distance countries there is limited dependence of subordinates on bosses, and a preference for consultation. . . . The emotional distance between them is (also) relatively small" (Hofstede, 1991, p. 27).

Consider some American students who have arrived to do their service-learning study abroad project on the Caribbean island of Trinidad; they expected they would be able to work directly with people in the community (i.e., low power distance expectations). However, soon after arrival, they discovered that the district leader, Don, expected them to get every single action cleared through him first (i.e., high power distance expectations).

This situation required an extra layer of communication before the community garden project could begin and necessitated additional conversations at each step along the way. Luckily for everyone, the local service-learning coordinator, Bula, was able to help the college students and the district leader find ways to communicate readily so the project could move forward quickly while the students were on the island. As a result of this work, the students and their professor looked forward to promoting "fair trade learning" (Amizade, n.d.) and began to work with Bula to plan a trip for local youth back to their home base so they could experience campus life firsthand. Importantly, this meant that the experience was not just "one-way," for college students to gain course credit, but instead created a win-win for everybody involved and helped support more equitable power arrangements between people at college and at the service-learning site. Because of the respectful way everyone involved him, Don got fully behind the effort and helped smooth the way for local youth to go back to campus a few months later.

Cultures also vary in how much they value feminine or masculine attributes and the behaviors traditionally assigned to each gender (Kurylo, 2013, p. 34). In a more masculine-oriented culture, for instance, emphasis is on power and external wealth as a means of dominance (Hofstede & Hofstede, 2005). On the other hand, in a more feminine-oriented culture there is greater equality and relationships are very important (Kurylo, 2013, p. 34).

Consider the experience of Cayla and Jose, who were classmates watching a show on television about traditions in Jose's native land of Mexico. Jose pointed out that it was highly acceptable for men to spar verbally to resolve a dispute, but women were expected to defer to their husbands. He didn't see this as problematic because it was the pattern he had always known. But Cayla came from a different cultural standpoint and questioned whether that approach was fair to working women. Jose hadn't considered that. In the end, their in-depth conversation helped them both to see that the impacts of the feminine-masculine dialectic were more complex than they had previously recognized.

Levels of tolerance for ambiguity, another cultural value dimension, involve how people manage situations of uncertainty. "People who feel threatened by ambiguous situations respond by avoiding them or trying to establish more structure to compensate for the uncertainty" (Martin & Nakayama, 2007, pp. 102–103). Stated differently, they show a low tolerance for ambiguity. In contrast, people in societies where uncertainty avoidance is not as much an issue tend to limit rules, accept dissent, and take more risks (p. 103). These individuals demonstrate a high tolerance for ambiguity.

An example of how this might work can be seen in the experience of Janine, who was anxious to learn about the organization where she would do her yearlong internship with Native Americans in another state. She scoured the Internet for details and sent e-mails and other correspondence to her assigned supervisor. Her interest was not only curiosity but also a willingness to take risks and seek more information showing her high tolerance for ambiguity between her own cultural background and what she might face on her internship.

Janine's supervisor, Black Elk, was very nervous about giving out any information about his people or the way his organization worked. He preferred to rely upon well-established, unspoken guidelines about how people worked together and wanted to meet Janine in person before sharing. His tendency to avoid uncertainty showed his low tolerance for ambiguity and meant that he didn't answer her e-mails or correspondence. Instead, he let her know that he would look forward to talking in person once she arrived.

These differences in their levels of uncertainty avoidance created initial tension between Janine and Black Elk. Still, both partners wanted to work together, so, given time and heart-to-heart sharing, they built a strong relationship and moved forward together.

Short-term or long-term orientation is somewhat like the dialectic of history/past-present/future detailed earlier in this chapter. Kurylo (2013) notes that

> countries which demonstrate a short-term orientation tend to prefer fast results and focus on social and status obligations. In contrast, countries that have a long-term orientation tend to value patience and endurance that bring results over a long time, have low concern for status, and are willing to adjust to change. (p. 35)

Take the example of Keva, a community center nutrition coordinator, who had wanted to build a community garden program for years and saw the long-term potential of that kind of program for the local people. She thought people of all ages could work together to grow, harvest, and prepare healthy foods—so different from the fast food they typically ate. Keva was consequently really excited that Dr. Mica and his class were going to share their expertise about community-based nutrition. She couldn't wait to have them help plan the community garden together.

But Dr. Mica had other ideas. His tenure and promotion decisions were imminent. That meant he had to get research about community-based nutrition completed and published as soon as possible. He knew his publications would be sent out within the year to external reviewers to assess the quality of all his scholarship. As that process progressed, Dr. Mica's work would be evaluated and would weigh heavily on whether he would be able to keep his job—or not! Dr. Mica was focused on a short-term orientation dictated by the tenure process at his university.

When Dr. Mica and Keva began to talk about their goals, they were seemingly at odds. However, Keva was skilled at working through differences and decided to see if she could help Dr. Mica get the quick results that met his needs. She also sought a longer term commitment from him to put the community garden project in place. They talked about their unique needs and their differences in time orientations. They were eventually able to develop a plan that met everybody's needs.

Understanding recognized intercultural value dimensions is a great place to begin building greater cultural awareness. In addition, other key capacities, such as relational empathy, authentic listening, and flexible approaches in communication, serve us well when working with the diverse people in our communities.

Capacities for Intercultural Communication

Relational empathy, an idea developed by Broome (1991), helps us stay open to learning more. Relational empathy is more than just putting yourself in the other person's shoes. Instead, relational empathy involves creating a "third culture" (p. 243) with unique values and norms that may not have existed prior to the relationship. This mutual creativity comes through conversations that explore the meanings both partners previously held in order to create a new reality (third culture) together (see also Broome & Collier, 2012).

Another important capacity for working with different cultural backgrounds is authentic, mindful listening, as discussed in prior chapters. That is, when we bring our whole selves into the listening process, we can uncover commonalities and ways we can work with one another.

For example, offering silence (i.e., no verbal feedback) while the other talks can be a very important way to show empathy and caring. This approach can be particularly meaningful when one partner is under extreme stress either personally or professionally. So when Keva recognized that Dr. Mica was stressed, she quietly listened to what he was worried about. It was only after silently gathering information about his perspective that the conversation fully continued.

At times, when Keva did ask questions to clarify and learn or encourage elaboration, she purposely did not guide the conversation. This showed her interest in Dr. Mica, not in her own agenda. She found that open-ended questions using who, what, when, where, why, or how yielded rich information and allowed Dr. Mica to share openly. She also decided to use yes/no questions sparingly.

Another communication practice for building stronger intercultural relationships involves being willing to change course when communicating, quite like the adaptability discussed previously. Flexible intercultural communication "emphasizes the importance of integrating knowledge and an open-minded attitude and putting them into active and creative practice in everyday communication" (Ting-Toomey & Chung, 2012, p. 28).

In intercultural interactions, flexible communication involves acquiring detailed cultural knowledge to understand attitudes reflecting the partner's cultural background and thus develop skills in interacting with that particular cultural group. Flexible communication also involves applying appropriateness, effectiveness, and adaptability (Ting-Toomey & Chung, 2012, pp. 28–29) in interactions. Appropriateness refers to communicating in ways that align with cultural expectations for the situation. Effectiveness involves accomplishing the intended goals or outcomes while honoring the partner's cultural background. Adaptability means being willing to change one's own outlook or communication behavior. Then, the communication and language choices used when conversing reflect the overarching concerns of the partner and the partnership.

Culture and the Collaborative Communication Framework

Communication in intercultural partnerships can involve every single part of the collaborative communication framework—repeatedly. The following examples show some of the ways it can happen.

Connecting

When Resa went to college in a southern U.S. state, he noticed that the most common greeting was "Hey." At first, this confused his northern sensibilities because in his past that word was reserved for trying to get someone's attention quickly when something major happened. Resa also noticed that his more formal greeting of shaking hands with everybody he met didn't get the response expected on campus. By learning new information and putting it into practice, Resa became more proficient at connecting with others at his new college.

Conversing

Paco, the coordinator of environmental action, was accustomed to talking whenever he had something to say, even if that meant he interrupted the other person. That is, he was used to conversations being very fluid and unstructured. He quite naturally interrupted his new friend Gene when they were working to glean water samples at a local river. Then one day, Paco overheard Gene's friend comment about how rude Paco was when talking to Gene. Because the two had a good relationship, Paco talked to Gene about this. Gradually, Paco learned that a back-and-forth-style conversational pattern was the norm for Gene. In addition, Gene learned to be understanding if Paco got excited and interrupted him while they were working together.

Envisioning

Painting mental pictures through words was something that Meli did well. This came naturally to her because of her African storytelling heritage. Whenever she wanted to get an idea across to another person, she thought through the best words to convey the image she wanted to share. Then one day, she met Emily, her new office mate at the Global Switchboard. (Learn about the Global Switchboard at http://theglobalswitchboard.org)

Meli approached their first conversation as usual, carefully choosing her words to create a verbal picture of her wishes for the space. But Emily didn't get it. She wasn't used to creating mental pictures; storytelling was not a familiar approach for her. She asked questions, but that didn't seem to help either. Eventually, they created a new way, a third approach. Each one drew sketches or looked for images on Pinterest to share. Then they could talk about the pictures and come to a clear understanding about what they both wanted. In time, Emily learned to appreciate the rich verbal story-like pictures that Meli readily created. Their chosen visuals along with the detailed word explanations helped the two of them create a vision that was meaningful for others as well.

Committing

Paul, a local director of the Red Cross with a Hindu background, and Geneva, the director of the local blood bank born and raised in a Christian household, couldn't understand why they were having a problem. Paul kept telling Geneva that he was committed to making their intercultural/interreligious interactions work better and better. From his perspective, the nature of their backgrounds shouldn't have impacted their support for people in the local communities. But Paul didn't realize that what Geneva really wanted to hear was that he was committed to her as a friend and fellow professional and not just to their partnership work or to relatively abstract conversations about their respective backgrounds. She wanted to know that her own opinions and feelings mattered so she could be open with him. Finally, after experiencing some confusion, they discovered the underlying problem. Then they were able to resolve differences, commit to one another as well as to the joint work, and then move forward together.

Collaborating

Justin, an entrepreneur, and Wali, a computer programmer from campus, were not accustomed to working with others. Both had grown up in masculine-oriented households where the man was supposed to make all the decisions for everyone else to follow. But when they began to work together as partners building a global entrepreneurial company with students and other community members from different backgrounds, major clashes occurred. Justin and Wali weren't able to sort it out themselves but recognized that some problem threatened to make their entrepreneurial efforts fall apart. So they brought in a third party to help them understand the situation.

Carol, a skilled mediator, quickly realized that both Justin and Wali needed to expand their repertoires of communication knowledge and skills in order to work well as a team. She set up a schedule and devised specific exercises for the partners to practice in a neutral situation, without strong emotions present. It took some time and always seemed to be a work in progress, but eventually the budding company began to grow. Also, Justin and Wali became fast friends and their partnership was stronger because of all their shared experiences and the new third-culture-level understandings that developed over time. That is, they had both left their original cultural understandings and developed a new third culture in their entrepreneurial work together.

This chapter presents some foundational concepts about cultures and communication. But *really* getting to know a person from another culture involves ongoing learning. Collaborative communication across cultures is a crucial undertaking to survive and even thrive in today's rapidly changing world.

Spotlight: Storyscapes Project

"There are so many different people walking right beside each other daily with no idea of who that person is or where they are coming from or what's their story," says Isiahm, a participant in the unique Storyscapes project in Greensboro, North Carolina. "I walk right beside them and I still don't see them," he says. "That goes on both ends" because the other people don't know him or his story either.

The idea for Storyscapes started one day as Gwen rode her bike to work at the Interactive Resource Center (IRC). She realized that others were walking along the same road from local homeless shelters toward the IRC. Whereas the route meant coffee to her, she recognized that the route meant something quite different to the others. She began to think about the stories people she worked with every day would tell if given the right opportunity.

"People can write more than about being homeless. . . . There are always other stories," Gwen says. Storyscapes was born to give people opportunities to tell stories about specific places that mattered to them. These places were then marked on a map to share details with others.

To create the first map, large sheets of butcher paper and markers were put out on a table at the IRC. Gwen sketched in two downtown streets. Then guests were invited to draw in points that mattered in their daily lives. Included were places to eat a hot meal, to find a day's work, or routes to walk from place to place.

Participants were also invited to write a story about what one place meant and to create an art object to illustrate that meaning. The resulting stories and art pieces were installed at the place described and were marked on a master map.

"I never thought my writing was anything extraordinary, but they really made me feel like it was something," Isiahm points out.

Through Storyscapes he met Kathleen, a longtime community activist, advocate, and organizer in the city and now a doctoral student at the University of North Carolina (UNC)–Greensboro. "We went to Home Depot to buy some tools and a couple pieces of wood to construct the piece," he said. "We had dinner and worked on putting the piece together. At the time I was on the streets so it was fun to be invited into someone's home and to be welcomed, truly welcomed . . . to share stories and laugh. Just have a good time working together."

"We're doing art. . . . It's not going to put food in my stomach, it's not going to put shelter over my head. But, because the relationship is real and genuine, I'm more appreciative of that than when a person comes in, shakes my hand, or looks down on me while he has food in his hand," he says.

By spending time together and learning about each other more, they were able to "let ourselves into one another's lives on a personal level instead of just through Storyscapes," says Kathleen.

"A real good thing about these partnerships is that they just don't skim the surface," says Isiahm. "I often don't see the deep roots necessary for a real relationship (with others). The fact that they don't create real relationships takes away from their mission."

Storyscapes provides "great learning opportunities for all of us," Kathleen points out. "People learn how to write grants, to get money, to talk about what Storyscapes is, to be on the news . . . to facilitate meetings and come up with an agenda, to decide on next steps."

Isiahm says, "It's been a shared responsibilities thing. . . . Anyone willing to take initiative in it can be a leader." He continues, "Different people have got different talents and strengths so those are being used."

Gwen says, "We would love to add layers to Storyscape maps (by other people in the area). . . . IRC guests would be facilitators to future groups because they have done this."

"Storyscapes gives a person an opportunity to look at things from a different perspective," says Isiahm. "Story sharing really deteriorates a lot of ignorance. . . . At the end of the day we're all people and that's all that should matter."

Putting Chapter Ideas Into Action

Action for Partnerships and Teaching About Partnerships

1. Gudykunst (1998) says the following skills are helpful in developing greater intercultural communication competence: (a) mindfulness or an awareness of one's own communication and ways of interacting

with others, (b) cognitive flexibility to create new categories for thinking with openness to new information, (c) tolerance for ambiguity so that minimal anxiety is experienced in an unclear situation (so that it can be assessed), (d) behavioral flexibility in order to adapt and accommodate others, and (e) cross-cultural empathy that makes it possible to imagine how the other might think and feel (pp. 226–238). Given that list, how might you and your partner (or your students and their partners) address each of the items? Consider ways to practice each of these skills in the classroom before, during, and after an intercultural encounter. These might also be important topics for reflection and sharing.

2. Anne Frank (2017) said, "We all live with the objective of being happy: Our lives are all different and yet the same." That short quote could stimulate a class discussion about both differences and similarities between cultures. Alternately, it could be used to create a "learning conversation" between partners. Too often when there are tensions or expressed differences, the focus is on the challenges and divergences between us. But a very powerful way to overcome our differences and collaborate more fully can be to find "common ground" between all the partners involved. Students or community partners could begin to list or explore both commonalities and differences and, in doing so, be increasingly aware of the uniquenesses of their partnership and of each other. Similarly, the chapter's opening quote could guide discussion about how individuals' diverse backgrounds might actually benefit partnerships as well as our daily lives.

Action for Community-Engaged Scholarship

1. One type of boundary spanning could involve using cultural distinctions and similarities more effectively when working together. Key research questions might include the following: When working with this specific community, what boundaries need to be spanned with the community members culturally? What cultural boundaries need to be spanned across the community organizations and their norms and practices? Are there places where these varied boundaries intersect or diverge and what lessons about communication might there be for us?

2. The idea of dialectics dates back to the ancient Greeks and has recently been applied to meaning-making among competing discourses (Bakhtin, 1981), communication in interpersonal relationships (Baxter, 1990; Baxter & Montgomery, 1996), and interactions in community engagement

(Dumlao & Janke, 2012) as well as in intercultural communication as described earlier in this chapter. Potential research questions include the following: What applications of existing scholarship about dialectics could be applied to studying the complexity of cultures and their communication? What might dialectical thinking offer to both scholars and researchers interested in looking at the practicalities of communication work with diverse groups in our rapidly changing world?

3. Any of the cultural value dimensions could be studied in relation to community engagement work. For instance, does the individualism-collectivism dimension offer new ways to look at our community partnerships? Could some partners be more focused on their own work whereas others are naturally focused on the good of the community? Importantly, what techniques for effective dialogue could be employed to help address such differences in perspective? What clues are offered in existing research that could be applied in terms of community engagement?

7

DEALING WITH PARTNER DIFFERENCES AND CONFLICTS

Peace is not the absence of conflict but the presence of creative alternatives for responding to conflict—alternatives to passive or aggressive responses, alternatives to violence.

—Dorothy Thompson (journalist)

Conflict and struggles may not be comfortable, but they are inevitable in a partnership. Tension can show up as under-the-surface struggles or erupt as conflict any time partners have views that don't mesh well.

Interestingly, though, our struggles and conflicts often point toward ways we need to change or adapt to one another. In fact, psychologists, human development experts, and others say conflict often precedes change! It's up to us whether those changes are positive—or not.

Like the name suggests, "win-lose" conflict strategies refer to moves where one participant wins and the other loses. Such strategies forcefully push for what one person wants with little regard for the other partner or his or her concerns. Win-lose strategies typically use aggressive, coercive language and nonverbals that create a hostile relational climate. (This is true whether messages are sent via interpersonal communication or via social media.) In community engagement, win-lose strategies can harm partners, hurt members in the community, and derail the partners' joint work. (To proceed, relational repair work may be needed.)

In contrast, "win-win" strategies balance individual concerns and needs with those of the partner. These strategies use supportive communication, listening and learning techniques, and methods to build a positive relational climate. Win-win strategies allow partners to work collaboratively despite expressed differences.

A Partnership Approach to Managing Struggles and Conflicts

Conflict handled well can promote peace, build greater understanding, and create positive change in our partnerships and in our communities. That's not to say handling conflicts is easy. It's not. Conflict can be complex, messy, and cause major friction, sometimes despite our best intentions. When we are in conflict, our past histories, cultural understandings, prior conversations, and more can rise to the surface, making partner dialogue challenging.

As a result, managing conflict well takes courage. A partnership-based approach means suspending judgments about the other person and the meaning of his or her actions in order to learn more about why those words and actions happened. This involves listening and conversing with compassion as well as giving up some control in order to create new possibilities with the partner. Moving into the unknown with hope and compassion while continuing to work together *always* takes courage! Even if we falter along the way, realigning with what we are working toward together can help us overcome difficulties. It's not easy but potentially rewarding.

Partnership-oriented conflict practices are in stark contrast to the attention-seeking or take-this-one-step-and-fix-it-all strategies seen on television or in the movies. Real-world relationships take effort and ongoing communication to address multiple layers of meaning-making while simultaneously sorting out individual (and group) differences so we can build bridges between us.

About This Chapter

This chapter offers practical information related to struggles and conflicts. (There's plenty of scholarly literature elsewhere.) Highlighted will be the importance of communication, with a focus on supportive communication. The learning/protective mode continuum will show how partners can gauge their readiness to talk—or not. Ways partners can use the collaborative communication framework and other strategies to guide productive, respectful conflict-related conversations will be shared.

Throughout the chapter, sample partner conversations will illustrate key ideas. Overall, the chapter will take a partnership approach to help partners find ways to move past struggles and conflicts to make positive, peaceful changes in their relationship so they can work better together.

Communication and Conflict

Communication is central in conflict. We use communication to express struggles, to describe details from our own perspective, to learn from one another, to generate workable responses, and to cocreate change. Without communication, conflict stays hidden and often percolates under the surface to erupt without warning.

Not just any communication will do, though. Some helps. Some hurts. Supportive communication is valuable for addressing the strong emotions that can accompany conflict as well as for building trust and promoting positive changes. (See chapter 4 for more about supportive and defensive communication practices.)

In an example of how this can work in conflicts, consider Marc, who had arrived early at the office just in time to get a heated phone call from the shelter's main contributor. Telling Marc her family-owned business had lost money during the last quarter, she was cutting her shelter contributions in half for the foreseeable future. Marc thanked her for her ongoing support, regardless of the amount she could give, and wished her greater success with her business.

As soon as he hung up the phone, Marc looked at the budget and sighed. The *only* way he could deal with this immediate loss of funding was to eliminate Cam's interview program. But when he looked at the figures closer, he realized that he could keep paying Cam the same salary. At least there was that.

He picked up the phone and made a call. "Cam, I have some unsettling news. Can you come talk with me a few minutes so we can consider what we might do?"

When Cam arrived, Marc walked around his desk to sit next to him. Then Marc said, "Cam, you've done a great job with the interview program over the last 10 years. It's really made a difference! Many, many people have gotten higher paying jobs working with you. So, know that I value what you do."

Cam looked at Marc with a puzzled expression. He wondered when the bad news was coming.

Marc continued, "Unfortunately, I got a distressing phone call this morning. Our primary contributor pulled half her funding. That means the one program that will be eliminated, for now, is yours."

Cam gulped. This certainly wasn't a good way to start the day. He asked, "Does this mean I am losing my job? I have bills to pay, you know."

Marc leaned toward him. "No. I can reassign you so you can keep your job. I'm still trying to think of ways to bring in funds for your interview program. Don't have those answers yet, but I want you to know I'll do everything I can. Meanwhile, I'd like you to head up the food distribution program working with the food bank. It's not the work you love, but you will be good at it and I need someone there right now."

Cam felt blindsided, but he could see that Marc was trying to be supportive. So he asked, "Would it be all right if I took my lunch now so I can go for a walk? That way, I can begin to process this big change before we talk more." Marc agreed.

On his walk, Cam met Mae, his professor friend. When Mae saw him, she was surprised. Cam's normally smiling face looked sullen. She said, "What's up, friend? I've never seen you look this gloomy."

"Yeah," Cam said. "I got bad news and don't know what to think. Do you have some time to talk? Maybe over pizza?"

Mae laughed and said, "You 've got it. Pizza is my favorite food group!"

Once she found out what was bothering Cam, Mae responded positively, saying, "Cam, I teach public relations. One thing my students learn is fund-raising. Maybe they could work with you and Marc to figure out a way to support your program?"

Cam was amazed. He left their lunch feeling better and eager to talk to Marc. He wouldn't mind heading up the food distribution program if it wasn't a permanent thing. This might work out after all!

Even though supportive communication demonstrates receptivity to the other person, as shown in this story, there are times when it seems more natural to react using defensive communication instead. Defensive communication uses words that evaluate, control, show indifference, manipulate others, claim superiority, or state absolute certainty with no room for alternate views. Defensive communication protects us and preserves our thoughts, perspectives, positions, and emotions (which can be important). But defensive communication also puts up a "brick wall" so that the partner can't readily share. Consider how the previous example could have gone differently.

Cam was so angry he could hardly speak, let alone have clear thoughts. Marc, his supervisor at the shelter, had just ordered him into the office, saying, "Cam, our major contributor cut her donations. I have no choice but to eliminate your interview program."

Cam just stared back. He couldn't say a thing or he'd lose it. Marc continued, "I've managed to keep your job, but you're reassigned to the food supplement program, effective immediately."

Cam thought to himself, "That program is a Band-Aid; it doesn't fix the problem. Why can't Marc see how important my program is? It helps people get better jobs and be self-sufficient!" He muttered, "Right. That solves everything."

Marc heard him and said quickly, "Okay, that's enough! Take your lunch break—now. Then, come back here. I'm doing the best I can. You need to come to terms with this or lose your job!"

Cam fumed, stormed out of Marc's office, and kept walking. Who could eat at a time like this? Deep down, Cam knew he was reacting emotionally, not responding rationally. So he started running. His feet pounded the pavement. And he nearly collided head-on with Mae. They both slammed to a stop.

Mae shouted, "Hey, Cam! Watch where you're going! You nearly mowed me down!" Then she saw his scowling face and slumped shoulders and knew something was really wrong. "What happened to you?" she asked.

Before she could utter another word, Cam yelled back, "They cut funding for my program! I've got a job, but not one that matters! Anyone with a lick of sense could run that food program!"

Mae heard part of what Cam said and responded, "Yeah. I know how you feel. My research budget got slashed last week."

That didn't help a bit. Cam said, "Really. I tell you about my problem and you tell me about losing research funding. Not the same at all." He thought, "I gotta get out of here." And he started running again. Mae stared after him, shaking her head.

Even after his run and talk with Mae, Cam didn't feel better. He now had full responsibility for running a program he didn't care about. He'd also been rude to Mae. (She didn't deserve that.) And Marc was just doing his job.

Cam's internal conversation continued. "Dang, the people I know and love are coming tomorrow to talk about interviewing. They will be soooo upset! I can't believe I'm going to let them down."

Fortunately, after she'd calmed down and thought a bit more, Mae decided to call Cam that evening. "Hey, friend," she said. "How about we get some pizza and talk about what's happening with you?"

So they got together, ate, and began to brainstorm ways to work together. Mae thought Cam could work with her students to raise more funds. After their dinner, Cam felt better and looked forward to talking to Marc first thing the next day. At least there could be a better conversation before he met with his clients to share the bad news.

Though exaggerated in this example, defensive communication between Marc and Cam began to escalate the situation into a full-blown conflict. This snowballed when Cam met Mae. Unfortunately, Mae initially reacted rather than listening, making things worse.

But Mae was also a skilled conflict manager and, given a little time, she was able to set aside her own concerns to listen carefully at the pizza place. She stated aloud things that she shared with Cam (i.e., common ground) to rebuild a strong connection between them. From that common base, they brainstormed (i.e., conversed) about ways to transform the emotion-charged conflict situation between Cam and his boss and to create new possibilities for the people they worked with every day.

Real Differences and Emotionally Charged Responses

Although supportive communication is very much needed by community-campus partners, poor communication isn't the only factor involved when conflict emerges. Conflict, by definition, involves real differences that need to be addressed (see Folger, Poole, & Stutman, 2001; Hocker & Hocker, 2001). Even if only one person "sees" the situation as a conflict, something needs to be addressed for reconnection and positive conversations to occur.

In addition, conflict can sometimes cause strong physical responses or internal tensions. Some research shows that we can be physiologically flooded in conflict. "You [can] reach the point when your thinking brain—the part that can take in gray areas, consider other sides, stay aware of the real state of affairs—is shut out. . . . [Such] emotional hijacking [puts] the nervous system in overdrive" (Manes, 2013). This is akin to what people call going into a rage when they can't see or think straight. That is what happened to Cam when he could only react and couldn't think clearly.

Taking time out to calm down and process things doesn't necessarily mean that we are running away from the problem. Instead, we may need to release tension through physical activity or change pace other ways. Taking time away can potentially allow us to be present for clear thinking and collaborative communication later. (If flooding or strong emotional reactions like overwhelming anger are an ongoing issue, professional help with understanding and managing the emotion-charged differences may be helpful.)

Short-term time-outs are quite different from telling ourselves that no real conflict exists and avoiding it permanently. When that happens, the conflict quite likely will emerge again—forcefully. So finding ways to address struggles or conflicts at the right time is crucial to our partnerships.

Learning and Protecting Modes in Conflict

One helpful way for each partner to determine whether he or she *can* converse fully is to quickly access his or her position on the learning/protective mode continuum. On the learning mode end, the partner is willing to connect to the other and have an honest, open conversation without holding back information or feelings. In learning mode the partner is in a good place mentally and emotionally and can be focused in the present and fully listen to the other.

On the protective mode end, the partner is *heavily focused* on protecting the self; the organization; and his or her interests, views, or positions, so walls go up and little information can be shared. The partner in protective mode might shut down and refuse to talk or might use uncharacteristically in-your-face, hurtful, and attacking communication—even might start avoiding conversations by missing meetings or making last minute changes in plans (see Lulofs & Cahn, 2000, p. 211).

As an example of using the protective mode and defensive communication, consider Jessy, who was really annoyed with Alex when they got into his car to go to the school carnival for their service-learning project. He had called her "lazy" and "unprofessional" because she hadn't returned his call the day before (i.e., Alex had used defensive communication).

Those words really hurt, so she shut down. She didn't want to talk to him at all (i.e., Jessy stayed in protective mode). Instead, she stared out the window. She couldn't believe Alex had used those hurtful words. She'd always thought she could count on him as a friend no matter what!

Deep down, Alex was confused. He couldn't figure out why Jessy didn't call him back like she always did. She'd let him down and he'd made a snap judgment that she'd acted unprofessionally. He'd said words without thinking (i.e., defensive communication). Things felt out of control. He needed to earn a very high grade so he could get into grad school. But that wouldn't happen if they didn't get to work on the project.

There was more to this situation hiding below the surface, though (as is often the case). Jessy had just learned that her beloved grandmother had died. She was in shock. She'd thought she'd still have years left with Granny. Jessy knew that if she said anything at all, she might break down sobbing uncontrollably. She couldn't do that at the elementary school.

Jessy just wanted to get done and wait for her father to arrive. She knew Alex was watching her and had no clue how upset she really was or why. But the words just wouldn't come.

When we are in protective mode like Jessy, we may not be able to converse at all, let alone have a learning conversation. When we are highly reactive or defensive like Alex, it's not a good time to talk either.

No matter how we get there, being deep in protective mode signals a need for self-care, self-reflection, and support. Sometimes being in protective mode can even signal the need to get safe physically—to get away from another person.

In this case, Alex and Jessy eventually resolved their issue. Once Alex found out that Jessy's granny had passed, he changed his thinking and became more supportive. He knew he would need to do most of the course project until Jessy was feeling better and could help. He sent her a quick text that said, "Hey, Jess, sorry to hear about your granny. That's tough! I'll pick up the slack while you are gone. Got you covered. Hugs!"

That supportive text was a beginning. Alex used a text to reconnect quickly and work toward repairing the relationship. Texting was a way they had often communicated before, and Jessy felt better as soon as she got the message. They both knew they could talk more later.

When partners can be present and listen with full focus on the words and attend to the nonverbals, they are at the other end of the continuum, in learning mode. Partners in learning mode are comfortable, able to relate to what's happening in the moment, and willing to listen flexibly for incoming information. Nonverbal postures are receptive, such as leaning forward or smiling or even reaching toward the other. Initial words shared indicate that the partner feels safe and ready to go.

Understanding where each partner is on the learning mode/protective mode continuum is important. Each partner can do a quick internal assessment using the learning/protective mode information. It's also really important to create a safe, comfortable place for both partners to converse. (See the appendix for more ideas.)

Creating a Safe, Comfortable Space to Talk

Imagine having a tough conversation about a struggle in a place where you feel scared or uneasy. The context could make you reluctant to share your true thoughts and feelings. In contrast, envision another place where you are comfortable and can readily express yourself. This space provides security for tough-to-have conversations that may come up.

Place matters when setting up partnership conversations. The best place is where *both* partners feel comfortable—a neutral or familiar location to all. The way furniture is arranged can also facilitate or hinder interaction. Using a circle encourages contributions from everybody. Separating people with a table or podium or putting them face-to-face does not. When two partners meet, a side-by-side or "around the corner" sitting style conveys equality.

When meeting for the first time, an agenda or list of "starter topics" can help partners know what to expect. Topic lists can be developed collaboratively using e-mail or something like Google Docs or OneDrive. This approach alleviates surprise or feeling blindsided; each partner has a chance to prepare.

Once partners meet (especially for the first time) an icebreaker or other fun activity helps form connections—for example, (a) use calm or culturally respectful music; (b) do a quick art project, especially one that is lighthearted or helps people "get out of their heads"; (c) share a reading that is inspiring, motivating, or focused on partnership or community building; (d) try a meditation or prayer that fits the people and the situation; or (e) begin with a calm breathing exercise. (See the appendix for resources.)

Once partners have worked together a while, they may develop quick "reconnecting" rituals that bring them together so they can get right to work. Remember in chapter 3 how Rocco and Gracie reached up and slapped hands to bond and reconnect so they could work together? That quick reconnecting ritual became a partner pattern. (See the appendix for more ideas about rituals.)

Before discussing serious matters, partners can set up a few ground rules for conversations. For instance, they can decide in advance what to do if things get tense or if a major struggle happens. (See the appendix for more.)

Let's put a few of those ideas into action by considering the example of Mae, who wanted Marc and Cam to come to campus to talk with her students, which in turn started a firestorm of concerns for the two men: Where would they park? What would it be like to stand in front of the students? How would they convey the seriousness of the work they did every day on the spur of the moment without a lot of visuals? Both Marc and Cam agreed that it would be better to have the students come to the shelter rather than to meet on campus, so Cam told Mae about their concerns.

Then Mae worked with her students to set up car pools to the shelter. Now the students were getting nervous. Many of them had never been "in that part of town." But when they arrived, Marc and Cam put everybody into a circle and immediately started throwing a beach ball back and forth. Whoever caught the ball would say his or her name and share one sentence about a favorite activity before throwing the ball to someone else. By the time this activity ended, everyone had shared a little, and laughter had eased the tension in the room.

Next, Marc explained how they worked at the shelter and brought in a smiling, elderly woman, Maude, who came to the shelter every day. Maude said in a booming voice, "Hey there, youngsters. I'll bet you haven't ever been here before!" (The students looked at each other, surprised to hear this.) "But, I'll let you in on a secret," Maude continued in a whisper. "This place used to be a dump, but Marc and Cam brought paint in and we all painted the walls. Then they brought in furniture that was not on its last legs. It's nice here now. And they are fun. I'm hoping you'll like it here enough to come back."

Everybody began to talk then about how they might help raise funds for Cam's program. Maude offered to be a "guest speaker" when meeting with potential sponsors. She said, "I love to speak my mind. That's what makes life exciting, and I know this place better than anybody else. Why I was coming to the dump even before Marc and Cam came around." By that

time, everybody was laughing and talking freely. This meeting was the beginning of many successful group get-togethers, both at the center and back on
campus.

Practical Strategies for Conflict Conversations

The collaborative communication framework offers a basic structure to use in
conflict communication. *Connecting*, as has been noted previously, is a critical step to getting ready before *conversing* about touchy or serious concerns.

Learning conversations can address key concerns in conflict through
"What happened?," feelings, and identity conversations (D. Stone, Patton, &
Heen, 2000). Each of these helps partners uncover what's going on for each
of them in order to hold difficult conversations. Such conversations can also
shed light on diverse perspectives, helping partners to address concerns and
make positive, lasting relational changes. (See the appendix for more ideas.)

Another approach, developed by Kare Anderson (1999), is called the
round-trip approach. This "powerfully simple 4-step method" is easy to
remember and apply, so it's useful in many different situations.

1. *Tell yourself the truth.* In the midst of heated reactions, Anderson says,
   "We need to slow down the process and seek personal clarity" by asking,
   What do I want? What's my bottom line? (Anderson, 1999, p. 23). Get
   as clear as you can inside yourself before proceeding. (This may require
   stepping back and taking time away.)
2. *Reach out to the other side* (in collaborative communication terms, connect more fully). While you do this, keep asking, "What is the other
   person's greatest need? What is most important to that person (as he or
   she sees it)?" (Anderson, 1999, p. 24). Anderson says these two questions
   are particularly important when the other person doesn't know what he
   or she needs most. In any case, don't assume you know what the other's
   needs are; keep exploring until the other person tells you.
3. *Listen attentively to the other side* and "demonstrate to that person that
   you have heard their concerns" (Anderson, 1999, p. 24) using respect
   and responsiveness rather than power plays. (See chapter 4 on listening.)
   "This (listening step) is often the most crucial time in a conflict, when
   your actions can either spark escalation or initiate a cooling off period.
   Don't rush or push now. The more you dislike the other side, the more
   time and effort you must summon to prove that you are indeed listening,
   that you are aware of their needs" (p. 24).

4. *Prove you are fair.* Address the other person's needs and interests first. "When you propose a solution . . . describe, in their language, how he (she) can benefit. Then you can discuss the benefits of such a resolution to yourself as well" (Anderson, 1999, p. 25).

In collaborative communication terms, the sequence of steps in the round-trip approach starts with *connecting* first with self and then with the other, *conversing* openly to include deep listening, and then continues by emphasizing *commitment* to the other person and the relationship (rather than focusing initially on your own needs). Once you follow those steps the partnership can be revitalized so you can begin to shift into *envisioning* new possibilities for working together (see K. Anderson, 1999).

Another approach to conflict conversations is the nonviolent communication process developed by Michael Rosenberg (2015) in conjunction with the Center for Nonviolent Communication. This four-part nonviolent communication process involves clearly expressing how "I am" without blaming or criticizing while also empathically receiving how "you are" without hearing blame or criticism (p. 231).

Step 1 has partners taking turns sharing observations without evaluation. State what is observed—without evaluation—from one's own viewpoint. "When I observe (see, hear, remember, imagine) . . . this does (or does not) contribute to my well-being" (Rosenberg, 2015, p. 231). Repeat these observations from the partner's perspective. (This is like supportive communication in chapter 4.)

For example, Hans, a graduate student, tells his community partner, Nora, "I saw you look at the ground when you talked with me the last time we met. . . . When I see a person do that I think they don't want to hear what I have to say so it stopped me from sharing with you." Nora responded, "I looked that way because I was trying to collect my thoughts. Now I understand why you didn't want to continue our conversation. Oh my!"

By describing the conversation without judgment, Hans presented Nora with the opportunity to explain why she looked down. This also allowed Hans to gather more information.

Step 2 involves each partner verbalizing feelings or emotions rather than stating thoughts. Each one can start with "I feel . . ."

Hans next said, "I feel really silly now. If I'd realized you just were trying to think clearly, I might not have felt sad because my thoughts were not welcome." Nora stated, "My intent was not at all to shut you down. I am also sad we had a misunderstanding."

Step 3 involves each partner stating needs or values rather than preferences or specific actions, using words like "because I need/value . . ."

Hans continued, "Now we know. I need to be comfortable with you and able to speak my mind." Nora responded, "Me, too. It's really important that we each feel free to discuss what matters most."

Step 4 involves each partner "clearly requesting that which would enrich my life without demanding" and "empathically receiving that which would enrich your life without hearing any demand."

So Hans might say, "Would you be willing to tell me if you are busy or preoccupied and can't continue to talk to me? That way, I won't think you are not open to me." Nora laughed and said, "Sure. That's easy. I am used to telling people when I have something else going on. You can count on me to do that with you!" (See the appendix for more ideas.)

There are a variety of ways to turn unproductive conflict situations into more productive ones using partner-focused communication. Once we have overcome a touchy conflict, we have reached a milestone. Later on, we can look back and remember how we traversed those past difficulties so we take heart in doing it again. Milestones can become partner reference points that help put a positive spin on what they can accomplish together in the future.

Putting Chapter Ideas Into Action

Action for Partnerships and Teaching About Partnerships

1. Using the two scenarios in the beginning of the chapter or another case study, have participants jot down the words or nonverbal communication that they think produced responses or reactions. (Table 4.2, about supportive and defensive communication, can help with this.) Then hold a discussion about supportive and defensive communication based upon these scenarios.
2. Take a conflict from real life or a movie and share with the class or group. Then apply one of the conflict approaches (round trip, learning conversations, or nonviolent conversation) to that situation. Then have a discussion about how this might work in a real-life interaction.

Action for Community-Engaged Scholarship

1. Vast literatures exist about conflict practices and processes in varied disciplines and from varied perspectives. Community-engaged scholars could benefit from doing in-depth literature reviews to glean practical strategies for further study of conflict. This could yield valuable ways to do

capacity-building for community and campus partners to better manage conflicts.

2. Conflict occurs at many levels of communication—between individuals, between groups, between organizations, between nations, and so on. Conflict between partners in community engagement work can reflect one or more levels. Scholars could identify conflicts that occur repeatedly between partners and develop a diagram or matrix to help pinpoint the levels involved in each. Such a detailed analysis could help to inform education trainings or other responses that have the most potential to benefit partners and their communities.

8

CREATIVE CHANGE FOR FUTURE COMMUNITY ENGAGEMENT

No matter what people tell you, words and ideas can change the world.

—Robin Williams (actor)

Throughout human history, people have successfully made big changes together, through communication and sharing with one another as well as through their combined actions. This remains true today!

Together, we can do what none of us can accomplish alone, even when responding to those people who seem to have greater power. Trying to respond individually—or in isolation—won't work. We need one another to create workable responses to the issues we face, to make positive changes happen.

The world has already changed in ways that can't be undone, pushing us toward more collaboration. For instance, social media and the regular inflow of information from around the world impact how we relate to one another—in our studies, in our work, in our communities, and in our homes. We are now aware of what is happening with people we might not have known a few years back.

Other communication technologies have changed our lives, too. In the United States, for instance, television viewers are no longer limited to three networks, as was the norm for prior generations. Instead, we have many media channels as well as a range of ways to watch. We may choose cable television. We may choose a digital antenna and subscriptions. We may choose satellite services. We can watch programs on a television, computer, tablet, phone, or even several devices at once. Similar changes are happening around the world.

The pace of change with media is both mind-boggling and exciting. Even while we are finding our way, new ways to share continue to develop. All these changes challenge us to identify effective ways to use the constant incoming content well.

Regardless of what medium we use to communicate, though, relationships matter. We can't live without them. So we would be well advised to choose our communication to build strong, lasting relationships—to collaboratively communicate.

About This Chapter

In this chapter you'll find information about creative ways to work together and share community-engaged work through storytelling, artwork, webinars, and short audios/videos. The chapter highlights the following important trends in community engagement: (a) international and global teaching and scholarship, (b) dialogue and bridging differences, and (c) entrepreneurship.

Throughout the chapter, tips about using social media will be offered. Additional suggestions will link the collaborative communication framework with fostering meaningful change.

Storytelling About Our Partnerships and Community Work

People have told stories throughout human history. Stories help us make sense of other people and what happens in life. Stories help us connect with our histories, our cultures, and our countries. Some experts even argue that stories form our sense of self and create basic meanings in our families (see McAdams, 1993; Pellowski, 1987; E. Stone, 1989; Turner & West, 2013).

Community engagement stories can impact others, too. These stories can include quotes (like journalistic stories) or creative writing elements. Regardless, our stories need to be compelling so readers, viewers, or listeners will pay attention. Using basic story elements is a great first step.

Most stories have a main character that sets up the action and "feel" of the story. Even when multiple people are involved, one main character often dominates. Think of your favorite children's book character and how the story seemed to be all about him or her. You probably connected with the story through the main character's personality or actions.

Another key story element involves posing a problem or a challenging issue. This is what the story plot is about—how the character deals with that problem or situation. In community engagement writing, we can highlight one aspect of an issue or a problem that could impact our audience.

An additional story element is the complication, an obstacle that gets in the way of the character solving the problem or addressing the issue. In the best community engagement stories, we identify (connect) directly with the complication(s) or we become really interested in what the character does to overcome that obstacle.

Once the complication is overcome the problem can be solved, the story often ends by recapping a lesson learned. When writing about community-engaged partnerships, this ending lesson pinpoints the knowledge or vision you hope your audience will carry away after finishing the story.

Sharing Our Stories via Multiple Media

Once developed, our stories must be shared in order to make an impact. Miller (2010) offers new realities to keep in mind for sharing stories and messages in today's media-rich world. Miller argues that there is no general public. She recommends focusing on specific groups of people, seeking to connect with their particular needs and values. (Audience analysis as explained in chapter 5 can help with this.)

How stories are shared matters, too. Different groups use different media, but not necessarily in ways we might expect. For instance, seniors are now online and increasingly using social media like Facebook. Miller thus contends that social media can help us connect with most people, not just with the younger generations. But social media use does vary by different user groups, so which social media to use to reach the intended audience is an important question to consider. (For more on social media trends, see M. Anderson & Perrin, 2017; Greenwood, Perrin, & Duggan, 2016.)

In addition, once separate functions (or former professional silos) of fund-raising, marketing, communications, and information technology are merging, says Miller (2010). Interestingly enough, she argues that "community building or community engagement teams . . . [that] incorporate all that is learned through their community of supporters into program design and implementation will ultimately be more successful in the coming years than those who maintain these professional silos" (p. 7). This kind of functional message merging is becoming a community engagement leadership capacity needed for the future.

Miller also notes that personal and organizational personalities or brands are blending. That is, those who most visibly carry messages to the public represent the overall emotional "feel" of an organization as well as what the organization "stands for." So, students, community engagement practitioners, and scholars need to know the mission and values their work represents and then develop messages and stories aligned with those priorities, commitments, and visions.

Having control over the message or stories is not possible, says Miller (2010), so "stop pretending otherwise" (p. 8; see chapter 2 for more on interpreting messages). "A more reasonable goal," says Miller, "is consistency in, rather than control of, your messaging" (p. 9). She also advises identifying controversial or hot button issues related to our work well in advance and determining how to respond to them. That way, the response can come quickly when these issues arise.

In sum, developing high-quality stories that influence others can be challenging. Practitioners, students, and scholars can consider effective storytelling another critical capacity to develop. Learning more about what to expect in today's media environment is crucial, too. We can work together creatively as we do this.

Artwork for Releasing Emotions and Working Together

Peanut butter, finger paint, colored chalk, and clay. More than items found in a preschool cupboard, artistic materials like these can help individuals tap underused creative qualities and bring out playfulness and fun. As adults, we often forget what it is like to unleash the freedom of expression that children take for granted. Caught up in our thoughts and busy schedules, we focus on other things. Still, creativity—including innovative solutions to problems—often begins when we let go and have fun by stepping outside our daily routines.

For instance, the author once watched a line of women run forward to throw clay balls as hard as they could while listening to energetic music. Each person yelled out a word or phrase for something she wanted to release. There was real satisfaction when that clay landed—*splat*—on the vertical wooden backboard! When all the clay was stuck on the board, the music was purposely changed to calm, melodious sounds to change the pace. Each woman took a turn etching and forming the clay into designs, figures, or whatever she wished.

After all had participated, formerly negative emotions were transformed. All the clay balls had been shaped into a group clay mural. Everyone participating stood back, looked at the result, and conversed about feeling lighter, freer, and more invigorated. Participating women also admired what they had collaboratively created.

This example of adult group artwork demonstrates one way to use art to transform emotions and form deeper connections between partners or within a group. Such a process might precede difficult conversations by helping release negativities before starting to talk in depth about a problematic situation. This creative process could also energize people to consider new visions for their future joint work.

Many other kinds of art could be used to enhance partnerships or community engagement work. The possibilities are endless. What can you imagine?

Music and Sound: Healing and Harmonizing

Music also holds powerful ways for us to relate to others. For example, "JazzLab is an exciting, enlivening, hands-on experience, using music making as a way to transform" (Tate, 2007, p. 593) your partnership, organization, or group.

Envision community participants in two large concentric circles around the edge of a room. After being encouraged to breathe, stay loose, jump in, and have fun, the group leaders establish rhythms using clapping and tapping, building from a single pattern to two parts, and then to four parts. After that, everyone plays the rhythm instruments they have made beforehand. Shakers, drums, scrapers, bells, and woodblocks are some options to use for the "artistic, mystic, rhythm orchestra . . . where everyone is discovering a new way of listening, getting 'in synch,' experiencing diversity in action and creating . . . synergy—where the whole is indeed greater than the sum of its parts" (Tate, 2007, p. 393).

JazzLab builds on the ideas that four primary elements of music are foundational for a holistic, healthy, and vital organization (partnership or group). Consider these elements:

1. While making music, we can listen deeply for long periods of time. This parallels deep listening in real-life interactions.
2. Following a common beat together provides a metaphor for having a common purpose and vision. Individuals play different parts or communicate in different ways, but hearing and synching with that common "beat" helps them work together.
3. Everyone's contribution matters in music. A wider mix of instruments adds texture to the sounds. Similarly, a mix of skills, personalities, and backgrounds provides a broad base for working together in community engagement efforts.
4. In music, we can hear and experience synergy, a tough concept to grasp conceptually. Even though the various instruments sound interesting solo in music, "when they come together, something wonderful is created that surpasses the mere combination of parts" (Tate, 2007, p. 395).

Notably, many of the music elements detailed are consistent with the community engagement values of equality, diverse voices, mutuality, reciprocity, and creation of relational synergy. In other words, blending parts equally, including different musical voices, and allowing each group or instrument to contribute in mutual, reciprocal, and synergistic ways can form delightful music. Also, using rhythm is one valuable way to connect with others without language or other communication inconsistencies. Through rhythm and music, we can be carried outside our thinking minds into new possibilities for creative changes—done together.

Webinars and Short Videos: Multisensory Ways to Share

Sometimes sharing information in our conversations doesn't meet all our needs. Webinars and short videos offer multisensory ways to share with our partners and communities to build capacities on varied topics.

Consider a webinar to be a seminar offered via video (or slides) to others over the Internet. Webinars can be viewed when convenient, across geographic and cultural boundaries. The widely popular TED Talks, for instance, share "ideas worth spreading" from experts on education, business, science, tech, and creativity in more than 100 languages. We can do something similar to share our community engagement work.

Webinars tend to be short, focusing on a key topic to "keep it simple" and exploring that topic fully. Watch a few TED Talks and you'll see how they are structured and personalized to make them compelling (see TED, n.d.). Thus, webinars are a great way to share information quickly.

Video meetings are another option. Unlike prerecorded, finished webinars, video meetings allow participants to interact in real time through a common website or software.

Notably, podcasts, as well as audio meetings or conference calls, can also help share information. These are limited to verbal cues so planning to share via podcasts or audio-only meetings would need to consider whether that limited incoming information would be sufficient for the purpose of the meeting or sharing.

Practically speaking, a variety of software is available to create webinars, videos, podcasts, or audio meetings; some are expensive. Check out what's available in your organization or through a quick online search. Truth is, a short video or webinar can be readily created on a cell phone. Or try using Gloopt online to create a story complete in under a minute. Similarly, audio recordings can be done on phones or using inexpensive equipment to later post online or share through e-mails or text messages.

Video and audio formats for sharing stories will continue to increase in value and importance in times to come. The best videos go viral—getting the story or message out to many, many people. News programs often pick these up and spread the word as well. Just think of the possibilities to do fund-raising, education, or calls for action using videos shared through multiple social media sites. Creative possibilities abound.

Collaborative Communication and Trends in Community Engagement

Our world is growing smaller, figuratively speaking. We readily connect with people at a distance, so *globalization* is more than a buzzword or passing trend. Global communication is today's reality. Global communication is also essential to bring about large-scale changes that extend beyond a specific locale.

Not surprisingly then, people around the world participate in community-campus engagement programs that benefit communities through teaching, scholarship, and service with others. Consider international travel as a way to propel yourself into international relationships and collaborative community partnerships away from home.

Dialogues across differences happen globally as well. Think of recent examples you've seen on social media or on television of people crossing boundaries in a positive way. Expanding your views to understand global perspectives could benefit many! (Find more about conversing across differences and managing tensions in chapters 6 and 7 as well as the appendix.)

Both locally and globally, a critical trend for community engagement work is to figure out how to be more entrepreneurial in our efforts. In short, we need new ways to support what we want to do with finances that don't originate solely on our campuses or community organizations. You've probably noticed that online fund-raising groups are popular. That's one possibility. (Search for fund-raising ideas online, for instance.) Another way to be entrepreneurial is to develop a product to sell with your community partners, ideally a natural extension of your work together. So, for instance, a community garden could offer produce to participants but also sell the excess in a farmer's market or to a local food supplier. New possibilities will continue to develop as funding shifts from government or single-provider sources toward more diversified funding streams.

A Few Final Thoughts

Collaborative communication is a necessity as you work together with your partners. We have an ever-increasing set of tools to connect, converse, envision, commit, and work to form partner patterns. (This book is just a start in learning to make collaborative communication part of your own community engagement projects. Watch for additional possibilities along your journey.)

You and I can make positive changes in a world filled with needs. Together we can create the kinds of sustained, positive change that are important to people in our communities—locally and globally. This work matters. We each have a vital contribution to make as we collaboratively communicate to benefit many!

Spotlight: Puppet Shows That Make a Difference

Puppet shows can be more than just fun, although they are that. Two college students from East Carolina University teamed up to create puppet scripts about important health topics to share with children near campus in Greenville, North Carolina.

These two students got started by taking an honors seminar, Puppet Shows That Make a Difference, from Deborah Thomson, a faculty member in the School of Communication. Class members learned to become masterful puppeteers working with specially designed Muppet-style puppets. The students also learned facts about healthy eating and diabetes prevention from an interdisciplinary team of experts. They then used this knowledge and additional research to create puppetry scripts designed for children in the community.

"I'd never done puppeteering before I started this journey," says Shayna. "Dr. T just made it. Day 1, she just let us jump in with puppets and theater games. . . . I've been stuck on puppetry ever since!"

Shayna and Teresa were so excited about puppetry that they continued to develop scripts on antibullying, healthy eating, dental hygiene, and exercise for almost three years after the seminar ended.

"Puppetry offers a fun, interactive way to get the material across," says Teresa. Children learn "what they can do at a young age to prevent health problems later on."

"The puppets are the perfect size for little kids," says Shayna. "You're not a scary teacher telling them this information. You're a fun, colorful puppet that moves and talks, telling them a story."

Teresa points out, "Anyone could stand in front of kids and say, 'You need to exercise and play 60 minutes every day.' But it's . . . different when the puppet is running . . . and you make the puppet out of breath, saying, 'Oh man, this is kinda hard. I should probably run some more' [to get in better shape]."

The children are "learning how to take care of their teeth from the dental scripts," says Shayna. "They're learning if you hurt someone's feelings, apologize. And how to breathe right while exercising. . . . They're learning things that they might not have gotten elsewhere."

The two puppeteers got to know some kids well. Shayna says, "We saw the same kids multiple times because we saw them at Little Willie (afterschool program). We went to their schools. We went to the Boys and Girls Club."

Their involvement with the kids didn't stop with puppet shows, either. Teresa invited 65 kids to campus for a Kids for Science Day, offering hands-on experiments run by 50 volunteers. Shayna designed and conducted a survey to find out whether kids learned about exercise better through a lecture style or via puppetry. Her honors thesis shared the results.

Both students understand more about collaborative communication from working with each other and with the children. Teresa learned "how to build off of Shayna's ideas and my own, merging those ideas in a way that will make sense to children." Shayna says, "It's interesting writing a script with a person when you don't know what they are thinking. . . . So you have to work together and get this cohesive script written out."

"In the long run," Shayna states, "everything is about working with others. You just have to be able to collaborate." She offered a few tips for working with others: "Any interaction you have anywhere, you have to go in with an open mind. You have to go in and work with them, not just for them . . . so you are working together. Even if you are doing a service for someone else, you can always be learning from them as well."

Author's Note: For more about using puppetry to reach community audiences and also increase college students' learning, see Thomson and colleagues (2016).

Putting Chapter Ideas Into Action

Action for Partnerships and Teaching About Partnerships

1. Practice zeroing in on a story. Have students or others write about a partnership in a journal or blog using the story elements listed previously. Also, have them consider that different stories have different purposes. Knowing the specific reader and the purpose (see chapter 5) are also important. Also, resources in the appendix can help you develop stories that build influence (Butman, 2013), that resonate (Duarte, 2010), and that help you and your partners become more memorable and quotable

(K. Anderson, 2014a), among others. Story-writing classes or workshops could be a great time to have an established writer come and talk. It's also a great time to ponder the sage advice of former Emmy-winning journalist Kare Anderson: "Share the story in which others see a role they want to play so they'll re-share it to make it 'our' story" (Anderson, 2014a). Alternately, just for fun, try developing a TED Talk to share online. Reviewing some inspirational TED Talks in a class or partnership workshop could be a valuable first step toward pinpointing the basic structure and then innovatively creating the script for a TED Talk. After that, videotaping the talk and posting it online could be a valuable way of sharing the work being done. (Tapping into campus resources in broadcast journalism or media production might be useful in getting this version of the learning activity accomplished.)

2. Help students or others learn to use select social media well. Consider ways to develop integrative approaches to get a main message out consistently (see LePage, 2017, and Smartsheet, n.d., for free templates to help with social media planning). In a class or workshop, take one or more of these templates and use them to practice ways to share a specific, focused message. This could be done in small groups around different messages or with all small groups working on the same main message and then making comparisons across the groups. This class or workshop would be a great opportunity to bring in someone who uses social media at work as a special guest. The topic could even build into a valuable workshop series shared across a campus or jointly offered in the community by a community-campus team.

Action for Community-Engaged Scholarship

1. Two-time Pulitzer prize winner Jon Franklin has written and taught that a single story should be developed using three complications (see Franklin, 1994, or the shorter interview of Franklin by Soennichsen in Franklin, 2004). Other writers use a series of stories that explore different aspects of a topic over time (which could focus on varied complications). Research related to the best ways to write or otherwise share complex stories around issues that have multiple "complicating" factors could prove valuable for community engagement work. An initial research question might ask, What are the best ways to share information so a specific target group or audience learns about a complex topic? Consulting the extensive communication literature about media campaigns or about

communication that impacts a particular group on a problem or an issue would be important in this scholarly pursuit.

2. A focused literature review of trends that could impact future community engagement work would be valuable to scholars and community partners alike. One way to start would be by generating a set of key words like *community trends* and *community engagement innovations.* Such a systematic search would be a great project for a community-campus research partnership.

Learning Activities

Connecting: Icebreakers

Icebreakers are like party games for connecting with a new person. Here are some to try the next time you meet with a new group of partners:

- *Wearing signs.* Before meeting, prepare a large note card or piece of paper with the name of a famous person or television character (it could even be a cartoon character). The person wearing the sign can't look at the sign but needs to guess what it says by asking questions. The others involved can't tell the wearer what it says but can only answer questions.
- *Post-its and sense-making.* In advance make several sets of Post-its using one color for nouns, another for verbs, a third for adjectives, and other colors for adverbs and other parts of speech. Then on a wall or a table, group all the same color together. After that, each person takes turns forming sentences with the words that are available. This can be used to explain how one feels *or* what one would like to see in the future (*or* ???). This is a way to get people to communicate when they don't really feel like talking to one another yet!
- *Similarities/differences interviews.* Have enough interview sheets for everyone. On the interview sheet, write down (a) things that can be observed like eye color, facial hair, wearing a watch, eyeglasses, and color of clothing; and (b) things that require conversations like place of birth, number of siblings, and favorite vacation spot. Have each participant use the interview sheets to find (a) someone who is just the same as him or her and (b) someone who is different. This is a great prelude to talking about similarities and differences in a nonthreatening way.

Connecting: Hold a Puppy or Kitten Event

Plan a special time when partners can visit with puppies or kittens. This gives everybody permission to get out of their heads and feel. Talking about feelings or dreams is a little more likely then. This kind of event could precede discussions or a workshop on emotional intelligence.

Connecting: Visit a Playground

Similar to the puppy/kitten event, going to a playground invites playfulness and talking about something other than facts, figures, and other verifiables.

Connecting: Take a Walk Together in Nature

Walking not only is great exercise but also can provide a way to get out of the normal work settings and tap into sensory information. Partners can naturally chat about what they see, hear, smell, and so on as they walk together. It's also a great way for some people to share without needing to constantly "look into one another's eyes."

Conversing Activity

Before starting a new conversation with a partner, imagine you are trying to gather the most insightful and fascinating information about this person in order to tell this person's story to others and really get everybody engaged with one another. Then plan a few intriguing open-ended questions (or request statements) like the following: What was your favorite memory as a child? If you could travel anywhere starting tomorrow, where would you go and why? Tell me about a time when you *knew* you were at your very best. Share with me something that you think is memorable about you. And so on.

Conversing: Surroundings

Making observations and sharing them in a meeting setting is an easy way to get a conversation started in a neutral way. For instance, you might wonder how the room was designed and who designed it. Or comment about the arrangement of the furniture and how that might facilitate communication (or not). Or look out the window and note the things within view. The idea here is to get a reaction and to encourage the other person to chime in and talk about the setting. Then it's often easier to shift to talking about the other person. For instance, if you talked about a classroom, a next line in the conversation could be about when you each are taking a class there.

Envisioning: Drawing When Brainstorming

Find a student artist or cartoonist to put a brainstorming meeting into pictures. (This could be a great addition to the student's art portfolio.) Using visuals along with words is a great way to tap into both crystalline and fluid intelligences.

Envisioning: Linking Ideas Visually

Put key vision ideas into circles and link them in different ways (similar to mind mapping). You can use free Prezi (Prezi.com) for this or Diagrammer (Duarte.com) to try out different ways of relating concepts to one another.

Committing: Identifying Key Elements

Partners may differ on what is most important in their commitment to one another, to the partnership, or to the community. Hold conversations about some of the key values, attitudes, and practices that each partner sees as "essential" for each of these. Consider words/phrases like *loyalty, interdependence, authenticity, sharing,* and *dealing with tensions.* (Try to think of more.) Use such words/phrases to talk more deeply using examples, descriptions, or even stories to explain what each one means to *each* partner.

Extend this conversation further using metacommunication. That is, talk about what communication practices best show values, attitudes, and so on. This is one way to come up with an initial set of communication processes and practices suited to this particular partnership (that can be changed over time to suit the people and the situation).

Partner Patterns: Keeping Track

Partner patterns typically take time to develop (or recognize) because they are unique to a specific partnership. So as partners meet, they can periodically point out things that (a) one partner loves about the other, (b) that one loves about this partnership, and (c) a partner would most like to offer the partner or partnership.

Partner Patterns: Possibilities

Partner patterns are indications of a past, present, and future. For instance, partners can develop special words or phrases or even nonverbals that are unique to their relationship. Examples include touching one's nose for "on the nose," showing a good fit for the partners when something worked well. Or a hand grasp and light hugs when partners meet as a way to check in. Partners can choose to use a visual image or wording on clothes or other wearables. Examples include a shirt with a logo designed by students in a class for the partnership, or a special cloth wristband created by a community group for the partners.

Additional ideas about partner patterns have been borrowed from some meaning-making practices used by other long-standing relationships like families (see Turner & West, 2013, on themes, rituals, metaphors, and stories).

- *Theme.* Recurring pattern that shows shared views or ways of dealing with things that happen. Partner talk will often reflect the theme. Examples: "We will stick together no matter what." "As partners, we can do together more than either of us can do alone."
- *Ritual.* Unique practices and communication events that focus on the partners, an idea, or the partnership itself. Examples: Having a quarterly or yearly celebration of milestones accomplished by partners; setting a monthly coffee and conversation meeting for partners to get together and enjoy one another's company without focusing on their joint work.
- *Metaphor.* A linguistic comparison of the partners to some other thing or object. Examples: "We work together like a well-oiled machine." "Our partnership is like a garden, with both weeds to be removed and flowers to cherish." "The sky is the limit, just like the many possibilities in our partnership."
- *Stories.* Shared memories or common experiences can provide stories that help bond and build a partnership over time. Stories can cover a range of topics or situations to include event-related happenings, funny situations faced, conflicts or struggles that have been overcome in unique ways, and so on. One way to pinpoint stories that matter to partners is to use start prompts such as the following: "Remember the time that we . . ." or "It makes me laugh every time I think about how you . . ."

Collaborative Communication Framework Skits

Using the collaborative communication framework illustrated in Table 3.1, work with class or workshop participants to brainstorm situations that use the elements of the chart. That is, brainstorm a situation that fits with connecting and another that fits with conversing, and so on. Then, working in groups, have participants develop two skits for each element—one that is positive and one that is negative. Act the skits out and then discuss the elements more fully.

To extend this activity further, choose one of the following topics covered in the book to explore "what happened" in the skits and how that led toward the outcomes: supportive versus defensive communication, meta-communication, paraphrasing (for a conversation), or mindful versus mindless listening (Turner & West, 2013).

A Spin Around the Framework

Sometimes when we face a new situation, we may not know exactly what to say. So at the beginning of a new community-engaged research project or at the beginning of a new service-learning class, take a spin around the framework.

1. Talk generally about the intended purpose of the community engagement activity and the community partner(s) involved to get familiar with what might happen during the class or the semester. (Ideally, the community partner could be involved in the discussion and the spin.)
2. Choose a major topic to consider related to the class or workshop. Describe it as clearly as possible. (A case study could serve this purpose.) Picture putting that topic in the center of the framework where the spokes meet. (For a workshop, a larger version of the visual might be helpful for all to see.)
3. Do a spin around the framework. Consider each element as it relates to the topic (and vice versa). Ask how the topic might impact connecting. Then ask how connecting communication might impact the topic. Continue around the framework until all elements have been considered. Pause to consider ways the elements may be interrelated when it comes to the topic.

Note: An alternative would be to use a current situation that needs to be addressed within a community-campus partnership as the topic in the middle and then do a spin around the framework. Many times this kind of deep exploration of a topic or situation will help uncover blind spots or new ways to communicate between partners.

Collaboration Checklist for Service-Learning and Engagement Projects

Throughout your service-learning/community engagement projects, you'll want to work together as a team with everybody involved. This involves both a collaborative mind-set and the use of specific team-oriented communication skills.

Directions: Put a + where you have well-developed skills now, an X where you have some abilities but could still improve, and a – in areas where you definitely want to improve.

Category 1: Join With Others
Take a relationship mind-set in all your interactions.

_____ Use "we" not "I" language.
_____ Totally avoid "us" versus "them" language!
_____ Seek common interests; talk about what you share or have in common.
_____ Acknowledge strengths and areas of expertise of everyone involved.
_____ Consult with others about your ideas, strategies, and so on *before* acting.
_____ When you talk, move closer to one another and/or lean in (to show interest and involvement).
_____ Keep in touch with others regularly to give progress updates.
_____ Work to build positive professional relationships with everybody.

Category 2: Control the Process, Not the Person(s)
Often difficulties can be alleviated or minimized with effective communication that is clear, inclusive, and team oriented.

_____ Work to keep everyone working together rather than splintering off into competitive subgroups.
_____ Choose meeting settings and timing to accommodate everyone as much as possible.
_____ Work to keep everyone informed, even if some are unable to attend meetings.
_____ Determine the "best" channel for communication for every interaction, whether e-mail, phone, text messaging, face-to-face, or other. (Think especially about whether nonverbal communication—body language, vocal tone, and so on—will be needed for clear understanding of messages.)
_____ Either limit or increase the number of people involved to get the job done.

_____ Encourage others to talk fully and share details in depth.

_____ Listen actively to what others are saying even if you disagree.

_____ Check out your assumptions as you go along. Don't assume you know what others are thinking or perceiving.

Category 3: Use Constructive, Productive Communication

Constructive communication helps build a supportive climate for your work.

_____ Be unconditionally constructive with all you say!

_____ Use supportive language rather than defensive language.

_____ Refuse to sabotage the process of problem-solving; stick with it!

_____ Separate the person or people from the problem.

_____ Choose persuasive communication to make your point rather than coercion or forcing.

Category 4: Be Firm With Goals but Flexible in How They Are Achieved

Things happen and your plans may need to change. Persevering with a flexible "can do" attitude will see you through to the completion of the project or experience (and is a most valuable career/life skill).

_____ Talk about your goals for the project or experience and get specific in what you are trying to accomplish.

_____ Set a list of criteria for your "ideal" end project or experience.

_____ Check in with everybody to get buy-in as you make decisions before you finalize project goals or ideal project/experience criteria.

_____ Work toward your goals but be ready to be flexible in getting there when new information or resources come into play.

_____ Separate content related to the project from any relationship issues.

_____ Focus on interests in the situation, not on positions people hold.

Category 5: Assume There Is a Solution for Every Challenge

Possibility thinking can carry you toward new options and creative solutions.

_____ Invent options that point toward win-win solutions.

_____ Reframe or change the way you are looking at the situation if necessary to come up with a creative but doable solution.

_____ Approach issues or concerns one at a time.

_____ First, tackle any issues or concerns that you can easily agree on; then, address those that are more contentious.

_____ Refuse to be pessimistic.

_____ Seek help if you or your group get stuck in any way.
_____ Know that you're in it together with the rest of the team.
_____ Celebrate your accomplishments and problem-solving.

Copyright 2009, Rebecca J. Dumlao

Cultivating Nurture Norms

Janke (2009) coined the term *nurture norms*. This variety of supportive communication can be important to the partners and the partnership and helps build a positive relational climate.

In a service-learning classroom or in a community partner workshop, try using a whiteboard or flipchart to post questions like the following: What are some of the things that you can do to nurture the other partners and the partnership as a whole? What "feels" nurturing to the different people here?

Have a discussion around what's practical and doable on a regular basis when working with your partners. (You are likely to identify personal or maybe even group differences for what nurture norms might work best.) Then draw or find pictures or words for the nurturing ideas raised and put them on a poster for future reference. This can be an incentive as well as a reminder about ways this class or workshop group chooses to work together well. And a quick phone picture can be a takeaway reminder when the group is no longer in session.

Learning to Self-Monitor in Communication Contexts

Self-monitoring or monitoring communication is useful in varied communication contexts. Noticing how we communicate while we are actually in the process of communicating can be a way to help make choices for communication practices (rather than to act based on habit or default).

Start with an easy-to-read book. (Children's books work great for this.) Then have each participant read a few pages while "self-monitoring." At least one other participant is to watch carefully while the reader is working. Then, after the first reading, have the reader state what he or she noticed about his or her verbal and nonverbal communication while reading. The other participant can also share observations. This can be repeated with the other partner reading. Or the first reader can try reading again, adding more variety or spice as if trying to interest a child in the book. Then again have participants talk about their self-monitoring or observations.

The idea is to practice self-monitoring when in a friendly situation so it becomes familiar. Then the process can become easier to use when getting a less desirable response from someone else. Self-monitoring allows us to make changes in how we are communicating verbally and nonverbally to try to get different results from another person.

Practicing Descriptions and Interpretations

An important skill in communicating more competently is to learn to distinguish between descriptions and inferences. For instance, in tense or conflictual situations, our perceptions or perspectives are colored by the inferences we make, which in turn influence our communicative responses.

Definitions

A *description* is an objective or neutral accounting of what happened. It sticks with the facts that others can observe or hear, like speaking loudly or crossing one's arms. Descriptions aim to be as accurate as possible in terms of what was observed or heard. There is *no judgment* included at all.

An *inference* is the meaning or interpretation or judgment assigned to those observations, like assuming that speaking loudly equals anger or that crossing one's arms means the person is not willing to communicate. (Loud speaking could also reflect the speaker's inability to hear something *or* it could mean that the speaker's primary cultural background promotes loud speaking as a way to assert power. Similarly, crossed arms could mean that the person is nervous or even cold.)

The Activity

1. Have everyone view a short video clip, a scene from a TV show or movie, an extended commercial, or a TED Talk.
2. Then without discussing anything, have each person take a piece of paper and fold it in half lengthwise. At the top of the left side, write, "Description." At the top of the right side, write, "Interpretation."
3. Give everyone time to write down *quickly* what they just observed as a description in the left-hand column. (*Do all of the left descriptive column first!*) One set of prompts for encouraging description uses the senses: What did you see? What did you hear? What did you smell? And so on.
4. Then have everyone write down their interpretation (what the description meant) in the right-hand column next to the various descriptions.
5. Exchange papers and let everybody read them quickly.

6. Begin a discussion about the distinctions between *descriptions* and *inferences* (using the definitions described in the previous section). Check to see whether any interpretations, meaning-making, or even judgments slip in inadvertently in the left column. Talk about how communication isn't always clear-cut. (You can refer to the transactional model of communication from chapter 2 and consider how the different parts of that model were demonstrated when the interpretations were made.)

7. Ask participants about their insights as a result of completing this activity.

Note: Although videos work well because they include both verbal and nonverbal cues, a similar activity can be done with only audio recordings. This could lead toward a discussion about the kinds of interpretation that could be done with videos versus audio-only sources.

Trust (and Repair Work) Conversations With a Partner

Review the different types of trust from chapter 4. Have a conversation with your partner about the types of trust needed now or for the future of the partnership. Ask questions like the following: Which types of trust have we addressed in our partnership so far? Are there areas of trust-building that need work right now? Do we need to think about doing any "repair work" to build more trust? If so, what steps can we take? What steps can we begin to enact to build a strong foundation of trust for the future?

Leadership Development Essay

Think about what leadership means to you. Write a reflective essay answering the following questions to share with your professor (or your community partner): (a) What leadership style works best in different situations? (b) How does leadership make a difference in my life as a student? As a community member? (c) What can I do to enhance my own leadership capabilities in the near future?

In class or in a workshop, have a discussion about the leadership development essays. Zero in on what this group thinks is most important about leadership. This can be compared to what is included in chapter 5 on leadership or other sources.

ANNOTATED BIBLIOGRAPHY

On Building Influence and Sharing Information

Butman, J. (2013). *Breaking out: How to build influence in a world of competing ideas.* Boston, MA: Harvard Business Review Press.

This book promotes methods used by "idea entrepreneurs" to take an idea public and build influence for it. Butnam shows how to craft personal narratives with rich content and share those stories in many forms, to develop related real-life practices and to create "respiration" around the key idea so that others can make it their own. Content from this book fits many contexts to include community engagement and change.

Duarte, N. (2010). *Resonate: Present visual stories that transform audiences.* Hoboken, NJ: Wiley.

This book builds on Duarte's trendsetting approach to infusing presentations with visuals that help grab and keep listeners' attention. In this practical guide, she focuses on how to use persuasion to "resonate" with others to promote change. Compelling case studies help readers see how masters like Mozart, Hitchcock, and E. E. Cummings used visual stories to transform audiences into considering similar approaches in their own presentations.

On Change Processes and Practices

Brown, T., & Katz, B. (2009). *Change by design: How design thinking transforms organizations and inspires innovation.* New York, NY: Harper Business.

The authors argue convincingly that tapping into intuition, recognizing patterns, and focusing on emotional meaning and function can be integrated with rational, analytical processes in the design process. Applicable in a variety of settings, content from this book tells stories from the design company IDEO and other organizations so the reader can identify principles and practices for great design thinking to explore different possibilities, taking a broader and more inclusive view than many other approaches.

Holman, P., Devane, T., & Cady, S. (2007). *The change handbook: The definitive resource on today's best methods for engaging whole systems.* San Francisco, CA: Berrett-Koehler.

This book profiles 61 change methods, with many explored through case studies, frequently asked questions, details about responsibilities needed, conditions for success, and more. A comparative chart makes it easy to determine which approaches might fit the intended community or organizational setting. Useful for those looking for new ways to promote change.

Nunn, M. (2013). *Be the change.* Atlanta, GA: Hundreds of Books.

This inspiring book, edited by the former CEO of Points of Light, offers hundreds of brief stories of people bringing about change in their communities and in the world. Also included are websites and additional resources to help one proceed on a journey of service to benefit many.

On Collaboration and Partnerships

Harvard Business Review's 10 must reads—On collaboration. (2013). Boston, MA: Harvard Business School Publishing.

The 11 articles in this compilation have a decidedly business bent. Still, there is much here to think about in terms of collaboration as it relates to social intelligence, leadership, boundary spanning, and conflict. This book could be particularly valuable when carrying on cross-disciplinary discussions about collaboration. It might also be the springboard for additional research about collaboration as it relates to social entrepreneurship and/or community engagement.

Heath, R., & Frey, L. (2004). Ideal collaboration: A conceptual framework of community collaboration. In P. Kalbfleish (Ed.), *Communication yearbook 28* (pp. 189–232). Mahwah, NJ: Lawrence Erlbaum.

In this chapter, the concept of community collaboration as distinct from other forms of collaboration is considered. The conceptual framework emerges from the bona fide group perspective and the systems perspective. This framework helps conceptualize collaboration, organizes the relevant literature, and suggests directions for research, especially about the constitutive role that communication plays in community collaborations.

Koschman, M., Kuhn, T., & Pfarrer, M. (2012). A communicative framework of value in cross-sector partnerships. *Academy of Management Review, 37*(3), 332–354.

The central argument is that cross-sector partnerships have value for organizations and for addressing complex problems, not just because they connect interested parties but rather in their ability to act by influencing people and issues. This comes about, the authors argue, from how organizations are constituted in forms that display collective agency—the capacity to influence relevant outcomes beyond what the individual organizations could do. Their framework shows ways organizations are constituted through communication processes and ways to increase and assess "value" through communication practices.

Lewis, L. (2006). Collaborative interaction: Review of communication scholarship and a research agenda. In C. S. Beck (Ed.), *Communication yearbook 30* (pp. 197–247). Mahwah, NJ: Lawrence Erlbaum.

This chapter reviews 80 sources from the prior decade about collaboration in various micro to macro contexts to include doctor-patient communication, health-care teams, community groups, and interprofessional and interorganizational settings. Themes in the literature along with definitional issues are developed and discussed. A descriptive, heuristic model of collaborative interaction is presented along with research and theory-building agendas.

Markova, D., & McArthur, A. (2015). *Collaborative intelligence: Thinking with people who think differently.* New York, NY: Spiegel & Grau.

Building on research in cognitive neuroscience, this book explains the collaborative-intelligence quotient, a measure of a person's ability to think with others on behalf of what matters to all. Four patterns are explored: mind patterns, the unique ways a person processes information; thinking talents, specific ways of approaching challenges; inquiry, the way a person frames questions and considers possibilities; and mind share, the mind-set shift required to align with others. This book could help partners explore their thinking processes related to collaborative communication.

On Educational Innovations

Rendón, L. (2009). *Sentipensante (sensing/thinking) pedagogy: Educating for wholeness, social justice, and liberation.* Sterling, VA: Stylus.

In this book, Rendón offers "a transformative vision that emphasizes the harmonic, complementary relationship between the *sentir* of intuition and the inner life, and the *pensar* of intellectualism and the pursuit of scholarship; between teaching and learning; formal knowledge and wisdom; and between Western and non-Western ways of knowing." The resulting pedagogy encompasses wholeness, multiculturalism, and contemplative practices so students can transcend limited views about themselves to foster high expectations and become social change agents.

On Leadership

Fairhurst, G., & Connaughton, S. (2013). Leadership: A communication perspective. *Leadership, 10*(1), 7–35.

This article reviews the literature on communication in organizations most relevant to leadership. The six value commitments of a communicative orientation, which cross several theoretical paradigms, organize this article and the research agenda that follows.

McKee, A., Boyatzis, R., & Johnston, F. (2008). *Becoming a resonant leader: Develop your emotional intelligence, renew your relationships, sustain your effectiveness.* Boston, MA: Harvard University Press.

This workbook shares information and activities for readers to grow as resonant leaders. Included are self-reflections, stories, and research about what great leaders think, feel, and do. Readers can also build capacities for mindfulness, better understand their own strengths and values, and create a vision for intentional change in the future. The last chapters share techniques for creating resonance with others and for sharing one's vision to impact others in positive ways.

Schmitz, P. (2012). *Everyone leads: Building leadership from the community up.* San Francisco, CA: Jossey-Bass.

This book focuses on several ideas—about leadership as an action everyone can take, not a position few hold; about taking personal and social responsibility to work with others on common goals; and about engaging diverse individuals and groups to work together effectively. Infused with stories and suggestions for learning about leadership and working with communities, this book could stimulate thought and discussions related to community engagement.

Whitney, D., Trosten-Bloom, A., & Rader, K. (2010). *Appreciative leadership*. New York, NY: McGraw-Hill.

This book approaches leadership through the lens of appreciative inquiry, focusing not on what's wrong but on what works. Five processes to get results with "positive power" are delineated: inquiry, leading with positive questions; illumination, bringing out the best in people and situations; inclusion, engaging with others to cocreate the future; inspiration, to awaken the creative spirit; and integrity, making choices for the good of the whole. Key practices, recommended books and websites, and many stories and reflection questions are included to facilitate this holistic approach to organizational or community transformation.

On Managing Conflicts or Struggles

Cupach, W., Canary, D., & Spitzberg, B. (2010). *Competence in interpersonal conflict* (2nd ed.). Long Grove, IL: Waveland Press.

This book presents a conceptual framework for why communication competence is crucial to conflict management. The authors say conflict is natural to the human condition and note that no checklist can guarantee success. Still they offer constructive guidelines to grapple with conflicts in different settings so that readers can begin to develop competent communication in intercultural, organizational, or family relationships. Included are useful concepts that could be used for discussion, practice, and community-engaged research.

Reimer, L., Schmitz, C., Janke, E., Askerov, A., Strahl, B., and Matyok, T. (2015). *Transformative change: An introduction to peace and conflict studies.* New York, NY: Lexington Books.

This easy-to-read text offers information to help promote change within groups or communities, despite conflicts and differences. Content about storytelling as peace-building, restorative processes and using artistic expressions to explore future possibilities could provide useful for classes or workshops. Valuable research ideas can also be found here. Indeed, one chapter focuses on engaging with communities for change and highlights key concepts from the community engagement literature.

On Managing Cultural Differences

Kim, M. (2002). *Non-Western perspectives on human communication: Implications for theory and practice.* Thousand Oaks, CA: Sage.

This scholarly book carefully explores the communication practices and related thinking processes of those holding "non-Western" perspectives. It could serve as an eye-opener to go beyond existing communication theories and best practices that are often based on a "Western" worldview and accompanying practices. It could also be used to help conceptualize more inclusive research and teaching.

St. Onge, P., Applegate, B., Asakura, V., Moss, M., Vergara-Lobo, A., & Rouson, B. (2009). *Embracing cultural competency: A roadmap for nonprofit capacity builders.* St. Paul, MN: Fieldstone Alliance.

This volume calls on capacity builders to "continuously seek to develop and improve their understanding of cultural competency and apply that learning to all processes . . . in which they are engaged" (p. 158). Conversations provide important tools for transformations and the chapters provided offer suggestions for doing just that. Also included are practitioner perspectives from multiple ethnic communities, key aspects of cultural competency development, and resources for continuing the conversation and building capacity for cultural competency.

On Social Media and Newer Forms of Communication

Bradley, A., & McDonald, M. (2011). *The social organization: How to use social media to tap the collective genius of your customers and employees.* Boston, MA: Harvard Business School Publishing.

Based on business practices of collaboration, this book zeroes in on ways to leverage social media to tap in to collective efforts. The authors identify core practices needed to turn mass collaboration into tangible results. Many examples and key questions are offered to show benefits and challenges of using social technologies. Practical advice and examples help show how you can use mass collaboration "to advantage." Useful techniques and insights could be applied to community engagement.

Miller, K. L. (2010). *The nonprofit marketing guide: High-impact, low-cost ways to build support for your good cause.* San Francisco, CA: Jossey-Bass.

This pragmatic, easy-to-read guidebook provides strategies, tips, tools, and resources to get the message out for your cause or organization. The author has also developed a website found at NonprofitMarketingGuide .com to offer additional resources, tools, and tips to supplement the book. Once there, readers can download a *Nonprofit Trends Report*, access the blog, secure free worksheets, and sign up for a free webinar on annual reports or an e-course on crafting better newsletters. Additional for-a-fee services can also be secured.

Web-Based Resources for Practice/Scholarship

Campus Compact, https://compact.org

This is a national coalition of 1,000+ colleges and universities committed to the public purposes of higher education in order to build democracy through civic action and community development. A national conference as well as information about localized events through affiliated regional or state compacts can be found. Syllabi by topic and discipline, news, blogs, a bookstore, and more can be located on the website.

Center for Creative Leadership (CCL), www.ccl.org

In addition to its training programs, webinars, and coaching services, CCL offers multimedia presentations, podcasts, white papers, articles, and other tools to help encourage leadership practices worldwide. Updates about their ongoing research projects on topics like millennials at work, gender perceptions related to leadership, and virtual teams are posted online. Researchers can access CCL assessments to study select leadership-related topics at a relatively low cost.

Center for Nonviolent Communication: A Global Organization, www.cnvc.org

Focused on making the world a more compassionate place through nonviolent communication (NVC) principles and practices, the website offers trainings and programs for individuals, educators, and families. Downloadable apps, CDs, written resources, and other tools to practice NVC are available through the website. The NVC Academy offers many additional subscription-based resources through a multimedia library (see https://nvctraining.com).

Civil Conversations Project, www.civilconversationsproject.org/
conversations/

This project seeks to renew common life in a fractured and tender world,
speaking together differently in order to live together differently. Taken from
episodes of *On Being* and moderated by Krista Tippett, these conversations
create space for a new quality of conversation and relationship, calm fears,
engage common life (even when common ground is absent), restore the
social art of listening, model adventurous civility and reframe entrenched
debates, and patiently call forth the best in ourselves and others.

Community-Campus Partnerships for Health, https://ccph.memberclicks
.net

This nonprofit membership organization promotes health equity and social
justice through community-campus partnerships. *Health* is defined broadly
as physical, mental, emotional, social, and spiritual well-being. The website offers extensive information, online networks, information about funds,
notes on conventions and meetings, and various toolkits. Particularly valuable is the Community-Engaged Scholarship Toolkit that can assist graduate
students and faculty to document their community-engaged scholarship and
produce strong portfolios for promotion and tenure. Also available is a data-
base of faculty mentors and portfolio reviewers.

Community Engaged Scholarship for Health (CES4Health), www.ces4
health.info/

The CES4Health website is a free online mechanism for peer-reviewing,
publishing, and disseminating products of health-related engaged scholarship that don't fit traditional journals. On this website, you can find videos,
manuals, curricula, and other products developed through service-learning,
community-based participatory research, and other community-engaged
work. Scholars can submit their products for vigorous peer review by both
community and academic reviewers; processes for review mirror those used
by most journals.

Consortium for Research on Emotional Intelligence in Organizations
(CREIO), www.eiconsortium.org

Intended to advance research and practice on emotional and social intelligence in organizations, this website offers practice guidelines; interviews
with key researchers; various emotional intelligence (EI) assessments; as well
as links to articles, technical reports, chapters, books, events, and a new video
series. Useful!

Design Thinking for Educators, https://designthinkingforeducators.com

IDEO Riverdale, an award-winning global design firm, contends that everyone can be part of creating a more desirable future and offers a creative process to take action and find meaningful solutions when faced with a difficult (or complex) challenge in the classroom, your school, or your community. Its website includes short videos, a toolkit, and information geared primarily toward K–12 educators but useful to others as well.

Global Service-Learning (GSL), http://globalsl.org

This research and "best practices" website offers a blog, research abstracts for books and articles, teaching tools and syllabi, a global citizen's guide, information about GSL Summits and other gatherings, and much more. It is a useful resource for anyone contemplating the start or expansion of a global service-learning program.

Imagining America, http://imaginingamerica.org/membership/

This organization brings together publicly engaged artists, designers, scholars, and community activists working to foster engaged scholarship, collaborative practices, and community revitalization and problem-solving that draws on arts, humanities, and design. Various publications hosted via the website share both innovative practices and scholarly information. Project stories are highlighted. Information about the national conference is also available.

Moving From Me to We: Succeed and Savor Life With Others, www
.sayitbetter.com/moving-from-me-to-we/

Kare Anderson, an Emmy Award–winning journalist, focuses on innovative, practical ways to be more quotable, connected, and collaborative. Her website offers a blog with practical, useful tips from the latest research and books, one-minute videos about key practices, links to her inspiring TED Talks, a free download on *34 Ways to Be More Widely Quoted and Deeply Connected*, and more. Highly recommended!

National Coalition for Dialogue and Deliberation (NCDD), http://ncdd
.org

NCDD is "a network of innovators who bring people together across divides to tackle today's toughest challenges." The website offers a blog and several e-mail lists, as well as a digital storytelling tool to help spread the word about your partnership successes. Confab calls are times to connect, learn, and hear about exciting projects. Tech Tuesdays are hour-long events to learn about using online technology for engagement. Links to partnering organizations and information about the yearly conference and other events can also be found here.

National Issues Forums Institute (NIFI), www.nifi.org

NIFI is a nonprofit, nonpartisan organization that promotes public deliberation about difficult issues. Deliberation is a long and careful consideration or discussion that thoughtfully weighs options to discover a shared direction guided by what is most valued. Resources available to assist in the deliberation process include listings of network partners/forum moderators/conveners for forums, as well as forum starter kits, issue guides, national reports, videos, and information about their conferences and gatherings.

National Youth Leadership Council, www.nylc.org

This organization is geared toward creating a more just, sustainable, and peaceful world with young people, their schools, and their communities through service-learning. The website offers several useful toolkits; custom trainings; conferences; and other resources like tip sheets, a blog, and online newsletters.

TakingItGlobal, www.tigweb.org

This is a global network of more than 500,000 young people learning about, engaging with, and working toward tackling global challenges to help shape a more inclusive, peaceful, and sustainable world. Resources on the website include discussion boards in multiple languages, online newsletters, downloadable action guides, toolkits, and publications from around the world, as well as information about a variety of global issues. Primary and secondary educators can register to develop collaborative projects through an online classroom platform and can find a variety of global resources for teaching as well as links to other organizations.

REFERENCES

Adler, R., Rosenfeld, L., & Proctor, R., II. (2007). *Interplay: The process of interpersonal communication* (10th ed.). New York, NY: Oxford University Press.

Altman, I., & Taylor, D. (1973). *Social penetration: The development of interpersonal relationships*. New York, NY: Holt, Reinhart, and Winston.

Amizade. (n.d.). *Fair trade learning*. Retrieved from https://amizade.org/consulting/ftl/

Anderson, K. (1999). *Resolving conflict sooner: The powerfully simple 4-step method for reaching better agreements more easily in your everyday life*. Freedom, CA: The Crossing Press.

Anderson, K. (2014a). *Mutuality matters: How you can create more opportunity, adventure, and friendship with others*. ebook: Substantium.

Anderson, K. (2014b, September). Opportunity makers have mutuality mindsets. *Moving From Me to We* [Blog]. Retrieved from http://www.movingfrommetowe.com/2014/09/15/opportunity-makers-have-mutuality-mindsets/

Anderson, K. (2014c). *Redefine your life around mutuality: Kare Anderson at TEDxBerkeley*. Retrieved from https://www.youtube.com/watch?v=FggFeSTr4Lw

Anderson, M., & Perrin, A. (2017, May 17). *Tech adoption climbs among older adults*. Retrieved from http://www.pewinternet.org/2017/05/17/tech-adoption-climbs-among-older-adults/

Astin, A. W., & Astin, H. S. (2000). *Leadership reconsidered: Engaging higher education in social change*. Austin, TX: ERIC.

Bakhtin, M. M. (1981). *The dialogic imagination: Four essays by M. M. Bakhtin* (M. Holquist, Ed.; C. Emerson & M. Holquist, Trans.). Austin, TX: University of Texas Press.

Barnlund, D. C. (1970). A transactional model of communication. In K. K. Serena & C. D. Mortensen (Eds.), *Foundations of communication theory* (pp. 83–102). New York, NY: Harper & Row.

Baxter, L. (1990). Dialectical contradictions in relationship development. *Journal of Social and Personal Relationships, 7*, 69–88.

Baxter, L., & Montgomery, B. (1996). *Relating: Dialogues and dialectics*. New York, NY: Guilford Press.

Bodie, G., Worthington, D., & Gearhart, C. (2013). The Listening Styles Profile-Revised (LSP-R): A scale revision and evidence for validity. *Communication Quarterly, 61*(1), 72–90.

Boyer, E. (1994). Creating the new American college. *The Chronicles of Higher Education, 41*, 48A.

Bringle, R., Clayton, P., & Price, M. (2009). Partnerships in service learning and civic engagement. *Partnerships: A Journal of Service Learning and Civic Engagement, 1*(1), 1–20.

Bringle, R., & Hatcher, J. (2002). Campus-community partnerships: The terms of engagement. *Journal of Social Issues, 58*(3), 503–516.

Brinkerhoff, J. (2002). Government-nonprofit partnership: A defining framework. *Public Administration and Development, 22*, 19–30.

Bronfenbrenner, U. (2009). *The ecology of human development: Experiments by nature and design.* Cambridge, MA: Harvard University Press.

Broome, B. (1991). Building shared meaning: Implications of a relational approach to empathy for teaching intercultural communication. *Communication Education, 40*(3), 235–249.

Broome, B., & Collier, M. J. (2012). Culture, communication, and peacebuilding: A reflexive multi-dimensional contextual framework. *Journal of International and Intercultural Communication, 5*(4), 245–269.

Burleson, B. R., & MacGeorge, E. L. (2002). Supportive communication. In M. L. Knapp & J. A. Daly (Eds.), *Handbook of interpersonal communication* (pp. 374–422). Thousand Oaks, CA: Sage.

Butman, J. (2013). *Breaking out: How to build influence in a world of competing ideas.* Boston, MA: Harvard Business Review Press.

Campus Compact. (2016). Who we are: Partnerships. Retrieved from https://compact.org/who-we-are/our-coalition/supporters-sponsors/partnerships/

Carriere, A. (2008). Community engagement through partnerships—A primer. *Metropolitan Universities, 19*(1), 84–99.

Carroll, G. (Producer), & Rosenberg, S. (Director). (1967). *Cool hand Luke* (Motion Picture). United States: Warner Brothers.

Centers for Disease Control. (2018). *High blood pressure.* Retrieved from https://www.cdc.gov/bloodpressure/

Clayton, P., Bringle, R., Senor, B., Huq, J., & Morrison, M. (2010). Differentiating and assessing relationships in service-learning and civic engagement: Exploitative, transactional, and transformational. *Michigan Journal of Community Service-Learning, 16*(2), 5–21. Retrieved from http://www.eric.ed.gov

Cooley, C. H. (1902). *Human nature and the social order.* New York, NY: Scribner.

Cutrona, C., & Suhr, J. (1992). Controllability of stressful events and satisfaction with spouse support behaviors. *Communication Research, 19*, 154–174.

Duarte, N. (2010). *Resonate: Present visual stories that transform audiences.* Hoboken, NJ: Wiley.

Dumlao, R., & Janke, E. (2012). Using relational dialectics to address differences in community-campus partnerships. *Journal of Higher Education Outreach and Engagement, 16*(2), 79–103.

Enos, S., & Morton, K. (2003). Developing a theory and practice of campus-community partnerships. In B. Jacoby (Ed.), *Building partnerships for service-learning* (pp. 20–41). San Francisco, CA: Jossey-Bass.

Ernst, C., & Chrobot-Mason, D. (2011). *Boundary spanning leadership: Six practices for solving problems, driving innovation, and transforming organizations.* New York, NY: McGraw-Hill Education.

Fitzgerald, H., Allen, A., & Roberts, P. (2010). Campus-community partnerships: Perspectives on engaged research. In H. E. Fitzgerald, C. Burack, & A. D. Seifer (Eds.) *Handbook of engaged scholarship: Contemporary landscapes, future directions: Vol. 2: Community-campus partnerships* (pp. 5–28). East Lansing, MI: Michigan State University Press.

Folger, J., Poole, M., & Stutman, R. (2001). *Working through conflict: Strategies for relationships, groups, and organizations* (4th ed.). New York, NY: Longman.

Frank, A. (2017). *The diary of a young girl.* New Delhi, India: Diamond Pocket Books.

Franklin, J. (1994). *Writing for story: Craft secrets of dramatic nonfiction by a two-time Pulitzer Prize winner* (reprint ed.). New York, NY: Plume/Penguin.

Franklin, J. (2004, November 18). Jon Franklin interviewed by Ole Soennichsen. *Niemann Storyboard.* Retrieved from http://niemanstoryboard.org/stories/an-interview-with-jon-franklin/

Frederickson, B. (2009). *Positivity.* New York, NY: Crown.

French, J. R., & Raven, B. (1959). The bases of social power. In D. Cartwright (Ed.), *Studies in social power* (pp. 150–167). Ann Arbor, MI: University of Michigan, Institute for Social Research.

Galvin, K., & Wilkinson, C. (2006). The communication process: Impersonal and interpersonal. In K. Galvin & P. Cooper (Eds.), *Making connections: Readings in relational communication* (4th ed., pp. 4–10). Los Angeles, CA: Roxbury.

Gardner, H. (2006). *Multiple intelligences: New horizons.* New York, NY: Basic Books.

Gibbs, J. (1961). Defensive communication. *Journal of Communication, 11,* 141–148.

Goleman, D. (2007). *Social intelligence: The new science of human relationships.* New York, NY: Bantam.

Gottman, J. (1993). *What predicts divorce? The relationship between marital processes and marital outcomes.* Mahwah, NJ: Lawrence Erlbaum.

Great! Schools. (n.d.). *Gatzert Elementary School.* Retrieved from https://www.greatschools.org/washington/seattle/1563-Gatzert-Elementary-School/#Students

Greenwood, S., Perrin, A., & Duggan, M. (2016, November 11). *Social media update 2016.* Retrieved from http://www.pewinternet.org/2016/11/11/social-media-update-2016/

Gudykunst, W. (1998). *Bridging differences: Effective intergroup communication* (3rd ed.). Thousand Oaks, CA: Sage.

Guerrero, L., Anderson, P., & Afifi, W. (2018). *Close encounters: Communication in relationships* (5th ed.). Los Angeles, CA: Sage.

Hackman, M., & Johnson, C. (2009). *Leadership: A communication perspective* (5th ed.). Long Grove, IL: Waveland Press.

Hardy, C., Lawrence, T. B., & Grant, D. (2005). Discourse and collaboration: The role of conversations and collective identity. *Academy of Management Review*, *30*(1), 58–77.

Harvard Business School. (2001, April). What makes a good leader? *Working knowledge: Business research for business leaders*. Retrieved from https://hbswk.hbs.edu/item/what-makes-a-good-leader

Hayes, E., & Cuban, S. (1997). Border of pedagogy: A critical framework for service-learning. *Michigan Journal of Community Service Learning*, *4*, 72–80. Retrieved from http://www.eric.ed.gov

Heath, R., & Frey, L. (2004). Ideal collaboration: A conceptual framework of community collaboration. In P. Kalbfleish (Ed.), *Communication yearbook 28* (pp. 189–232). Mahwah, NJ: Lawrence Erlbaum.

Hersted, L., & Gergen, K. (2013). *Relational leading: Practices for dialogically based collaboration*. Chagrin Falls, OH: Taos Institute Publication.

Hocker, W., & Hocker, J. (2001). *Interpersonal conflict* (6th ed.). New York, NY: McGraw-Hill.

Hofstede, G. (1980). *Culture's consequences: International differences in work-related values*. Beverly Hills, CA: Sage.

Hofstede, G. (1991). *Cultures and organizations: Software of the mind*. London: McGraw-Hill.

Hofstede, G. (2001). *Culture's consequences: Comparing values, behaviors, institutions, and organizations across nations* (2nd ed.). Thousand Oaks, CA: Sage.

Hofstede, G., & Hofstede, G. J. (2005). *Cultures and organizations: Software of the mind* (2nd ed.). New York, NY: McGraw-Hill.

Holland, B. (2005). Reflections on community-campus partnerships: What has been learned? What are the next challenges? In P. Pasque, R. Smerek, B. Dwyer, N. Bowman, & B. Mallory (Eds.), *Higher education collaboratives for community engagement and improvement* (pp. 10–17). Ann Arbor, MI: National Forum on Higher Education for the Public Good.

Holliday, A., Hyde, M., & Kullman, J. (2010). *Intercultural communication: An advanced resource book for students* (2nd ed.). New York, NY: Routledge.

Holman, P., Devane, T., & Cady, S. (2008). *The change handbook: The definitive resource on today's best methods for engaging whole systems* (2nd ed.). San Francisco, CA: Berrett-Koehler.

Humphrey, D. (2007). *Intercultural communication competence: The state of knowledge*. London: CILT.

Jacoby, B. (1996). *Building partnerships for service-learning*. San Francisco, CA: Jossey-Bass.

Janke, E. (2008). *Shared partnership identity between faculty and community partners* (Doctoral dissertation). Retrieved from http://etda.libraries.psu.edu/theses/approved/WorldWideIndex/ETD-2962/index.html

Janke, E. (2009). Defining characteristics of partnership identity in faculty-community partnerships. In B. Moely, S. Billig, & B. Holland (Eds.), *Advances in service-learning research: Vol. 9. Creating our identity in service-learning and community engagement* (pp. 75–101). Charlotte, NC: Information Age.

Johnson, C. (2001). *Meeting the ethical challenges of leadership: Casting light or shadow.* Thousand Oaks, CA: Sage.

Keyton, J., & Stallworth, V. (2003). On the verge of collaboration: Interaction processes versus group outcomes. In L. R. Frey (Ed.), *Group communication in context: Studies of bona fide groups* (2nd ed., pp. 235–260). Mahwah, NJ: Lawrence Erlbaum.

Komives, S., Wagner, W., & Associates. (2009). *Leadership for a better world: Understanding the social change model of leadership development.* San Francisco, CA: Jossey-Bass.

Kotze, M., & Venter, I. (2011). Difference in emotional intelligence between effective and ineffective leaders in the public sector: An empirical study. *Informational Review of Administrative Sciences, 20,* 397–490.

Kress, G. (2010). *Multimodality: A social semiotic approach to contemporary communication.* New York, NY: Routledge.

Kurylo, A. (2013). *Inter/cultural communication: Representation and construction of culture.* Los Angeles, CA: Sage.

Lavenda, R., & Schultz, E. (2010). *Core concepts in cultural anthropology* (4th ed.). New York, NY: McGraw-Hill Higher Education.

LePage, E. (2017, June). *7 Social media templates to save you hours of work.* Retrieved from https://blog.hootsuite.com/social-media-templates/

Lewis, L. (2006). Collaborative interaction: Review of communication scholarship and a research agenda. In C. S. Beck (Ed.), *Communication yearbook 30* (pp. 197–247). Mahwah, NJ: Lawrence Erlbaum.

Lulofs, R., & Cahn, D. (2000). *Conflict from theory to action* (2nd ed.). Needham Heights, MA: Allyn & Bacon.

Manes, S. (2013). *Making sure emotional flooding doesn't capsize your relationship.* Retrieved from http://www.huffingtonpost.com/stephanie-manes/relationship-tips_b_3676764.html

Markova, D., & McArthur, A. (2015). *Collaborative intelligence: Thinking with people who think differently.* New York, NY: Spiegel & Grau.

Martin, J., & Nakayama, T. (2007). *Intercultural communication in context.* New York, NY: McGraw-Hill.

Mattessich, P., Murray-Close, M., & Monsey, B. (2001). *Collaboration: What makes it work (A review of research literature on factors influencing successful collaboration)* (2nd ed.). St. Paul, MN: Fieldstone Alliance.

McAdams, D. (1993). *The stories we live by: Personal myths and the making of the self.* New York, NY: William Morrow.

McCornack, S. (2013). *Reflect and relate: An introduction to interpersonal communication* (3rd ed.). Boston, MA: Bedford St. Martin's.

McKee, A., Boyatzis, R., & Johnston, F. (2008). *Becoming a resonant leader.* Boston, MA: Harvard University Press.

Miller, K. L. (2010). *The nonprofit marketing guide: High-impact, low-cost ways to build support for your good cause.* San Francisco, CA: Jossey-Bass.

National Communication Association. (2016). *Transactional communication model.* Retrieved from http://www.natcom.org/Tertiary.aspx?id=511&terms=Transactional Communication Model

National Communication Association. (n.d.). *Ethical statements.* Retrieved from natcom.org

Nunn, M. (2012). *Be the change.* Atlanta, GA: Hundreds of Heads Books.

Oyserman, D., Kemmelmeier, M., & Coon, H. (2002). Rethinking individualism and collectivism: Evaluation of theoretical assumptions and meta-analyses. *Psychological Bulletin, 128*(1), 97–110.

Pellowski, A. (1987). *The family story-telling handbook: How to use stories, anecdotes, rhymes, handkerchiefs, paper and other objects to enrich your family traditions.* New York, NY: Macmillan.

Phillips, G. M., & Wood, J. T. (1983). *Communication and human relationships.* New York, NY: Macmillan.

Pierro, A., Raven, B., Amato, C., & Bélanger, J. (2013). Bases of social power, leadership styles, and organizational commitment. *International Journal of Psychology 48*(6), 1122–1134.

Planalp, S., & Honeycutt, J. (1985). Events that increase uncertainty in personal relationships. *Human Communication Research, 11,* 593–604.

Potter, W. J. (2014). *Media literacy* (7th ed.). Thousand Oaks, CA: Sage.

Reina, D., & Reina, M. (2006). *Trust and betrayal in the workplace: Building effective relationships in your organization* (2nd ed.). San Francisco, CA: Berrett-Koehler.

Rosenberg, M. B. (2015). *Nonviolent communication: A language of life* (3rd ed.). Encinitas, CA: PuddleDancer Press.

Ruderman, M. N. (2011). Foreword. In C. Ernst & D. Chrobot-Mason (Eds.), *Boundary spanning leadership: Six practices for solving problems, driving innovation, and transforming organizations* (pp. xv–xx). New York, NY: McGraw-Hill Education.

Sandy, M., & Holland, B. A. (2006). Different worlds and common ground: Community partner perspectives on campus-community partnerships. *Michigan Journal of Community Service Learning, 13*(1), 30–43.

Schmitz, P. (2012). *Everyone leads: Building leadership from the community up.* San Francisco, CA: Jossey-Bass.

Seattle University Youth Initiative. (n.d.a). *2012–2013 annual report.* Retrieved from https://www.seattleu.edu/media/youth-initiative/files/results/impact/SUYI-Annual-Report-2012–2013-FINAL.pdf

Seattle University Youth Initiative. (n.d.b). *At a glance.* Retrieved from https://www.seattleu.edu/suyi/results/impact/at-a-glance/

Shearman, S. M., Dumlao, R., & Kagawa, N. (2011) Cultural variations in accounts by American and Japanese young adults: Recalling a major conflict with parents. *Journal of Family Communication, 11*(2), 105–125.

Shockley-Zalabak, P. (2015). *Fundamentals of organizational communication: Knowledge, sensitivity, skills, values* (9th ed.). Boston, MA: Pearson.

Siegel, D. (2010). *Organizing for social partnership: Higher education in cross-sector collaboration.* New York, NY: Routledge.

Smartsheet. (n.d.). *Free social media templates for Excel.* Retrieved from https://www.smartsheet.com/social-media-templates

Socha, T., & Pitts, M. (2012). *The positive side of interpersonal communication.* New York, NY: Peter Lang.

Stoecker, R., & Tryon, E. (2009). *The unheard voices: Community organizations and service learning.* Philadelphia, PA: Temple University Press.

Stone, D., Patton, B., & Heen, S. (2000). *Difficult conversations: How to discuss what matters most.* New York, NY: Penguin Books.

Stone, E. (1989). *Black sheep and kissing cousins: How our family stories shape us.* New York, NY: Penguin Books.

St. Onge, P., Applegate, B., Asakura, V., Moss, M., Vergara-Lobo, A., & Rouson, B. (2009). *Embracing cultural competency: A roadmap for nonprofit capacity builders.* St. Paul, MN: Fieldstone Alliance.

Tate, B. (2007). JazzLab: The music of synergy. In P. Holman, T. Devane, & S. Cady (Eds.), *The change handbook: The definitive resource on today's best methods for engaging whole systems* (2nd ed., pp. 593–597). Oakland, CA: Berrett-Koehler.

Taylor, P. (2014, April 10). *The next America: The new us.* Retrieved from http://www.pewresearch.org/next-america/

TED (Ideas Worth Spreading). (n.d.). *2600+ talks to stir your curiosity.* Retrieved from https://www.ted.com/talks/

Thomson, D., Dumlao, R., & Howard, J. (2016). Building civic capacity for college students: Flexible thinking and communicating as puppeteers, community partners, and citizen-leaders. *Journal of Community Engagement and Scholarship.* Retrieved from http://jces.ua.edu/building-civic-capacity-for-college-students-flexible-thinking-and-communicating-as-puppeteers-community-partners-and-citizen-leaders/

Ting-Toomey, S., & Chung, L. (2012). *Understanding intercultural communication* (2nd ed.). New York, NY: Oxford University Press.

Triandis, H. C. (1988). Collectivism and individualism: A reconceptualization of a basic concept in cross-cultural social psychology. In G. K. Verma & C. Bagley (Eds.), *Cross-cultural studies of personality, attitudes, and cognitions* (pp. 60–95). London: Macmillan.

Triandis, H. C. (1995). *Individualism & collectivism.* Boulder, CO: Westview.

Turner, L., & West, R. (2013). *Perspectives on family communication* (4th ed.). New York, NY: McGraw-Hill.

United Nations Population Division. (2014a, August). *Population facts: Our urbanizing world.* Retrieved from http://www.un.org/en/development/desa/population/publications/pdf/popfacts/PopFacts_2014-3.pdf

United Nations Population Division. (2014b, August). *Population facts: Population ageing and sustainable development.* Retrieved from http://www.un.org/en/development/desa/population/publications/pdf/popfacts/PopFacts_2014-4.pdf

Vangen, S., & Huxham, C. (2003). Nurturing collaborative relations: Building trust in interorganizational collaboration. *The Journal of Applied Behavioral Science, 39*(1), 5–31.

Waldron, H., Turner, C., Alexander, J., & Barton, C. (1993). Coding defensive and supportive communications: Discriminant validity and subcategory convergence. *Journal of Family Psychology, 7*(2), 197–203.

Walker, K., & Stohl, C. (2012). Communicating in a collaborating group: A longitudinal network analysis. *Communication Monographs, 79*(4), 448–474.

Warner, A. (Producer), Williams, J. H. (Producer), Katzenberg, J. (Producer), Adamson, A. (Director), & Jenson, V. (Director). (2001). *Shrek.* (Motion Picture). United States: DreamWorks.

Watson, K. W., Barker, L. L., & Weaver, J. B., III. (1995). The Listening Styles Profile (LSP-16): Development and validation of an instrument to assess four listening styles. *International Journal of Listening, 9,* 1–13.

Watzlawick, P., Beavin, J., & Jackson, D. D. (1967). *Pragmatics of human communication.* New York, NY: Norton.

West, R., & Turner, L. (2006). *Understanding interpersonal communication: Making choices in changing times* (2nd ed.). Boston, MA: Wadsworth Cengage Learning.

White, B. (2015, February). *Navigating the power dynamics between institutions and their communities.* Keynote presentation at the Pathways to Achieving Civic Engagement Conference, North Carolina Campus Compact, Elon University.

Wood, J. (2007). *Interpersonal communication* (5th ed.). Belmont, CA: Thomson/Wadsworth.

ABOUT THE AUTHOR

Rebecca J. Dumlao earned her PhD at the University of Wisconsin–Madison, is a professor of communication, and is passionate about service-learning and other forms of community engagement. She says, "I have always wanted to be a teacher who made a difference in people's lives." Early in her career she served as the director of a nonprofit health organization and worked as a freelance author, before shifting into academics.

She believes learning can be fun. So, she's worked with other faculty and community members to plan student-led workshops for communication capacity-building as well as puppet shows where college students shared information with children about healthy eating and lifestyles. She regularly presents and publishes on family communication, conflict communication, and community engagement topics in peer-reviewed academic venues and through community-based workshops. As a result of her ongoing efforts she has received the Robert L. Sigmon Service Learning Award from North Carolina Campus Compact and East Carolina University's Scholarship of Engagement Award along with several teaching awards.

Dumlao loves to travel and has taught in Trinidad, West Indies, and in Maastricht, The Netherlands, as well as in Wisconsin, Oregon, and North Carolina. She has worked with others to take students on an innovative service-learning trip to work with youth in Northern Ireland. In her spare time, she authors fiction, coaches about wellness and empowerment, quilts, gardens, and enjoys two small doggies, Dolce and Nani.

INDEX

Engaging Higher Education

Purpose, Platforms, and Programs for Community Engagement

Marshall Welch

Foreword by John Saltmarsh

"Rarely in a maturing scholarly field does a volume provide both breadth and depth of scholarship, but Marshall Welch's volume accomplishes this feat masterfully. This volume extends an evidence-based synthesis of how higher education systems structure and implement community engagement, as well as a 'how-to' for higher education institutions. It will serve multiple purposes for higher education administrators, faculty, community engagement center directors, and graduate students in education." — *Patrick M. Green, Founding Director, Center for Experiential Learning, Loyola University Chicago; Past Board Chair, International Association for Research on Service-Learning and Community Engagement*

For directors of campus centers that have received the Carnegie Classification for Community Engagement, this book offers research and models to further advance their work. For directors starting out, or preparing for application for the Carnegie Classification, it provides guidance on setting up and structuring centers as well as practical insights into the process of application and the criteria they will need to meet.

22883 Quicksilver Drive
Sterling, VA 20166-2019

Subscribe to our e-mail alerts: www.Styluspub.com

Also available from Stylus

Community-Based Research

Teaching for Community Impact

Edited by Mary Beckman and Joyce F. Long

Foreword by Timothy K. Eatman

"In an environment in which some governors insist a college's worth should be measured only by the number of graduates getting high-paying, high-demand jobs, this book reminds us that many students achieve a different kind of education: one that cultivates an ethos of investigative care about solving problems faced by the very communities in which they live and will work. That's the kind of education that really prepares graduates to be the workers our country needs: competent, collaborative, solutions-oriented, and invested in the greater good."—*Caryn McTighe Musil, Senior Scholar and Director of Civic Learning and Democracy's Initiatives, Association of American Colleges & Universities*

"*Community-Based Research* would be a good book for faculty members interested in designing community-based research (CBR) projects with students to enhance their learning and help them make connections between theory and practice. As Long acknowledges, 'there is still much more work to be done in documenting student outcomes linked to CBR,' but this book contributes to this ongoing research. The text is particularly effective in the way it accounts for the unique roles students have played in CBR (e.g., as a change agent, active citizen, allied community member, and coauthor). This book would also be a valuable resource for community members, students, and faculty members who want to work in solidarity with one another to strengthen the communities they share. It would also improve the lived conditions of one another and their neighbors both locally and globally."— *Teachers College Record*

(Continues on preceding page)